You are Loved!

Charles

COMIC BELIEF

Charles Lowery, Ph.D.

6Acts Press
Irving, Texas

Comic Belief

Charles Lowery

First edition – 2004
6Acts Press
2322 Creekside Circle South
Irving, Texas 75063
972.432.8690
www.6Acts.org

Printed in the United States for worldwide distribution
ISBN: 0-9703229-6-8

Dedication

To Penny – my friend, my wife, and the love of my life.

To my daughters and their husbands – Angela and Jon, Kasey and Brad, and Breanne and Paul, whom I am proud to say, continue the Lowery tradition that families of faith have a lot of fun.

To my grandchildren – Drew, McKenzie, Greyson, Jake, Cas, and Jackson, whose love and laughter assure me that there will be a Comic Belief Part 2.

To Tim Horner and all of the Horner family who have believed in and supported my gift of comic belief.

Thanks also to the Board Members of Life, Inc.:

Tim Horner
W. L. and Cynthia McCulloch
Terry and Pam DeLaPorte
Paul and Sharla Jones
Mark and Sandy Day
Debbie Orrell

Table of Contents

Foreword

Mickey Mouse Motivates

Behind the magic, the sparkle, the fantasy, fireworks, adventure, and discovery lies one of the most impressive showcases of management you will ever see – run by a mouse. I had the privilege of looking behind the Disney magic curtain by traveling to Mickey's domain and the famous "Small World" of Walt Disney World in Orlando, Florida. I learned some valuable principles of management that Mickey Mouse and his entire cast live by.

Disney World strives to understand the type of people it is attracting. The bottom line of Disney World's success is management by storytelling. People's lives are stories told by the things they say and the lives they live. Disney World says that success is achieved through successful relationships with people. To establish a good relationship with someone, you must understand his story.

Disney World achieves this success by putting its people through a management-training program that includes learning to tell and understand stories. For example, the trainee who will be in charge of the ride called Dumbo the Flying Elephant is trained not only in how to operate the ride but in how to "read" the people who are going to ride it. He learns about the little boy with leukemia whose last wish is to ride Dumbo the Flying Elephant. So when the operator sees a little kid in line, he doesn't just think about operating the ride, he thinks about the little boy with leukemia whose dream is to ride Dumbo the Flying Elephant.

The secret of Disney World is not the methodological and the mechanical; the secret is its focus on people and its understanding of the human spirit.

I have discovered that our personal success also lies in stories. True success in life is to fully live our own story and enable others to live theirs. We should all have stories to tell in our companies, our churches, our synagogues, and our families. Our lives should be stories in progress.

I have discovered that illustration is more personal than instruction. Stories make instruction personal, therefore more powerful. And humor is important, too; it moistens the needle and lowers the defenses.

So most of the stories in this book are jokes. They're really jokeries (a combination of jokes and stories). Since I first heard of most of these from other people, forgive me if I tell one of yours, and I will give you permission to tell some of mine. I hope you find yourself going from "ha ha" to "aha". Be careful; these jokeries could change your life.

1

Relating to Relationships

Most of the joy, and unfortunately most of the pain in life, is centered in relationships. First comes love, and then comes marriage and a lot of emotional baggage. Emotional baggage is similar to regular baggage. You don't realize how difficult and troublesome it is to haul around until you have to put it down. I hope these jokeries will lighten the load and make your journey brighter.

I Am Woman Hear Me Roar; I Am Man Tell Me More

A little boy who grew up in a town so small the school bus was a yellow Toyota went shopping at the town's drug store. The boy told the druggist he wanted three boxes of candy. He wanted a one-pound, a three-pound, and a five-pound box of candy, each box gift-wrapped. The druggist told him okay, then asked the girl behind the counter to wrap the boxes. When the candy was ready he told the boy, "Here are your one-pound, your three-pound, and your five-pound boxes of candy. I don't want to be nosey, but this is an unusual request. Would you mind telling me why you want three different sizes?" The boy replied, "I'm so excited, sir, I'd love to tell you. I have a date tonight with the cutest girl in the whole school. I'm going to her parents' house and have dinner, and after dinner we're going to go out on the porch and sit on the swing. And, sir, if she lets me hold her hand, I'm going to give her the one-pound box of candy. If she lets me put my arm around her, I'll give her the three-pound box of candy. And, sir, if she lets me kiss her, I'm going to give her the five-pound box of candy."

The boy arrived at the girl's house, sat down for dinner, and the father asked him to say the blessing. He prayed and prayed. He prayed around the world once and then again and then prayed some more. Finally he stopped and the girl turned to him and said, "I didn't know you were so religious." He replied, "I didn't know your daddy was the druggist!"

I can identify with that little boy. Relationships seem to get more and more confusing. A little girl and boy who had just met were playing. The boy said, "Let's play baseball." She said, "I don't want to do that. Baseball is a boys' game, and it's not feminine to run around in a dusty vacant lot. I'm not going to play baseball." He said, "How about football?" "No, that's

even less feminine. You have to fall down and get dirty. That's not a girls' game." He said, "Okay, I have an idea. I'll race you to the corner." She replied, "No, let's play a quiet game, a game where we don't run and get all sweaty. Besides, girls never race with boys." The boy scratched his head in confusion trying to think of something they could do. Finally he said, "I have it. Let's play house." She said, "Good, I'll be the daddy."

Relationships are confusing because we think we are normal and everyone else is weird. This attitude shows up in male/female relationships. Suddenly, your prize package has become a *surprise* package. I think the bottom line is that women are just more complex than men. I know my wife is. For example, if you look in my bathroom you will find about five items – toothbrush, toothpaste, shaving cream, razor, and maybe some hair spray. But if you look in Penny's, you'll find about 97 items, most of which I don't have a clue as to what they are. Then there's the closet. In Penny's closet are clothes, shoes, and a section for all of her purses. She has brown, black, multi-colored, spring, winter, casual, formal, and Easter purses. My closet, on the other hand, has no such section; I have only one wallet, and most of the time I can't find it.

I think, deep down, men are just shallow. A man can go on a vacation for a week and carry only one suitcase. He can go to the bathroom without taking a support group, and he can get a three-pack of underwear for less than $15. He can go to his friend's house without taking a little surprise gift. Men didn't grow up saying, "Let's go to my house and braid our hair and talk."

So, guys, take my advice. Learn to say just three little words that will revolutionize your relationship. When she tells you about the new color she's considering for the family room, just look in her eyes and say three simple words, "Tell me more." I guarantee you there will be less conflict in your house. And, ladies, remember that when your husband says, "Tell me more," he doesn't really want to know more. He is asking only

because I told him to, and he loves you. So think in terms of a pamphlet, not a novel. Keep it short with a lot of action, kind of like a Three Stooges movie. He will love it.

Feel My Muscles

Women have seven stages of life: infant, little girl, miss, young woman, young woman, young woman, and young woman. And any woman knows that the seven stages of a man are: infant, little boy, little boy, little boy, little boy, little boy, and little boy. Most smart women know that a man is just a ten-year-old boy all grown up. He still wants a woman to think he's wonderful. A ten-year-old boy is outside doing flips on the jungle gym for his mom. He says, "Mom, look at me. Aren't I strong? Feel my muscles." She agrees, "You are so strong. You're so wonderful." He always performs for his mother, and his mother always encourages him. But then something strange happens when he turns sixteen or seventeen years old. His mother starts to see the negative. Instead of watching him perform she focuses on the things he needs to improve. He says, "Feel my muscles." And she responds with, "Clean up your room," or "Make better grades."

Eventually he begins to look around for another woman. Ah-ha! "Feel my muscles. Aren't I wonderful? Watch how hard I hit the ball." The new woman says, "You're wonderful! Let me feel your muscles. You're so strong." They get married. But if this woman isn't careful, she will become like his mother and begin to focus on the negative. He still wants her to feel his muscles and tell him he is wonderful. What happens if she doesn't? He starts to look for another woman. Most affairs don't take place for physical reasons, but for psychological reasons. A man wants to hear that he's good and wonderful and the best.

I'm not the best speaker in the world, but when Penny and I go to a conference where I'm on the program with several others, she always tells me I'm the best. I like that. That's another way of saying, "Feel my muscles; aren't I strong?" That's what a man needs. He's just a ten-year-old boy grown up. He wants to be noticed. Every little boy wants to be a hero, and the way to his heart is through his ego.

A "thank you" a day will keep the lawyers away. Ladies, when was the last time you told your husband you appreciated him for all his hard work? Better yet, tell other people how great your husband is. You say, "Wait a minute, Charles; he's not very good." Let me ask you something. Why did you marry him if he's not very good? Did you look for someone who would make you miserable? Before you married, you convinced your parents how good he was. They may have told you that you weren't old enough or that they didn't like him, but you convinced them otherwise by telling them all the good things about him. What happened? Perhaps your husband isn't wonderful anymore because you don't say wonderful things about him anymore.

Start saying he's the best, and he will start acting like the best. There is one slight problem, though. He probably doesn't know how. He needs help, like a 10-year-old boy. Be specific. Don't just say that you like flowers; be specific. A hint such as "I like flowers" doesn't get the job done. That will go over his head, and he'll bring home a package of seeds. You have to look him in the eye, show him flowers, and say, "On the next special occasion, roses like that would be nice, and I especially like the yellow ones." Be direct. If you tell him that you like to travel, he'll come home with a road map. You have to say, "I want to go to the Grand Canyon with you." Romance to a man is a woman telling him exactly what she wants. That's freedom. He can accomplish what you want and ask you to feel his muscles. This approach applies to every area of life – communication, the physical, and the sexual. Men need specific directions.

Men hate to ask directions, but sometimes they must because they're as lost as a ball in tall weeds. They know they don't have a clue, so they do stop to ask directions; but, even then, male pride gets in the way. For instance, a guy will stop at a convenience store and ask the lady behind the counter for directions. "Do you know where Route 41 is?" She says, "Yes, it's easy to find. Go to the third red light and take a left. Then go around the curve, but don't take the next right. Go to the next right, and you'll see a big tree. Go past the tree and turn on the next left. Go about a 1/2 mile and on the left you'll see a big curve. Go past that curve and on past the next curve you'll turn left and you'll be on Route 41." Every man in America will say, "Thank you very much." He'll go back to his car and he won't have a clue where Route 41 is. His wife will ask, "Do you know where it is now?" And he'll say, "She didn't know." He drives on and won't ask again. There's not a man in America who will say, "Excuse me, you're going too fast. Could you slow down so I can make notes?" Now, if the lady behind the counter takes the time to show him, we're getting somewhere. She might say, "You know, I have to go right by there in just a few minutes. Why don't you follow me? I'll go slow, and when I honk the horn you'll be there. I'll turn the blinker on and you turn." The man would say, "Thank you, God." And he will find Route 41.

Ladies, this is how you work with a man if you want him to get somewhere; you have to take him slowly and be direct and specific. Remember he's a 10-year-old boy. If you tell him how to do it, he will. Why? So you can feel his muscles.

The Two O'clock Bus

A sports team was in the middle of a terrible losing streak when the manager called a meeting and said, "There will be two buses leaving the hotel for the ballpark tomorrow. The two o'clock bus is for those of you who need a little extra work. The empty bus leaves at five o'clock." In other words, everyone on the team needed a little extra work. Men also need to put in some extra effort, especially in the area of relationships.

It's not hard to find evidence that men have some shortcomings. Recently, without even trying very hard, I found three telling examples in the news. The first example was about a basketball coach who admitted to being "a little bit too focused." He said that when his young son was three years old, he took him to the barbershop so they could both get a haircut. While the coach was getting his haircut, he started focusing on a ball game on TV, and he continued to think about it as he went home. Two hours later, his wife came home and asked, "Where's Jeff?" Just then the barbershop called to say, "Jeff's read all the comic books that are here, and we're about to close. What should we do with him?" The coach realized he had left his son at the barbershop.

Then consider the 78-year-old man in Key West, Florida, who thought his roommate was just being stubborn by refusing to answer him. It turned out his roommate had been dead for two months.

A third example is about little Matthew Murray, who took the ride of his life. His daddy put Matthew in the car seat and placed the car seat on top of the car. Then Matthew's dad got into the car and took off. At fifty miles-per-hour, he saw a diaper go up in the air, and then he saw the car seat, with Matthew in it, fly through the air. Fortunately, the baby landed right side up in the median, and when his dad got to him, Matthew was smiling. Needless to say, God puts extra angels on duty when men are taking care of children. I heard about a guy who was baby-sitting twins. He fed the same one over and over and almost starved the twin brother.

That's the way men are. They focus on what they are doing and forget everything around them, especially relationships. When men my age were growing up, our hero was John Wayne. He said only two words – "Yep" and "Nope." That's all he said, and if *talking* didn't take care of the problem, then he would fight 'em or shoot 'em. He was our hero, and we follow his trail. We're like the man who told his buddy, "I had words with my wife; she had paragraphs with me."

Most men want to be close to a woman who will leave them alone. But a woman's heart is like a campfire. If you don't tend to it regularly, you'll soon lose it. It is a constant battle of balance. For example, women want romance. Romance is the opposite of practical. Women think roses. Men think, "Why invest in something that will be dead in four days?" It's not the flowers women love; it's the *feelings* they love when they receive flowers from *someone* they love. The flowers will die, but the feelings of love will live on, and that is worth your investment.

The concept of Valentine's Day is basically difficult, if not impossible, for men to grasp. I was speaking at a Valentine's Banquet for which the women had gone to a lot of trouble to create the right atmosphere. They decorated the gym and renamed it the "Love Café." It was romantic with music and candlelight. I listened to the comments from the men at the tables. They were saying things like, "I can't see my peas." "It's so dark in here, I don't know what I'm eating."

A Midwestern farmer placed an advertisement in a farm journal. "Wanted: healthy, wholesome wife to work on farm. Must have tractor. P.S. Please send picture of tractor." That's a guy – practical through and through. No wonder one lady said her husband had all the characteristics of a dog except loyalty.

Guys, we have to think differently. "Royal Dining" is not eating at Dairy Queen or Burger King. And she doesn't want a new set of tires for her birthday.

Let me give you some hints – assurance instead of answers, sympathy instead of solutions, and perfume instead of kitchen appliances.

For the guy who said, "I don't know what to get her for Valentine's this year – she hasn't used the floor sander I got her last year," look for the two o'clock bus. Believe me. You need the work.

Men

A few years ago the Forester Sisters sang a song about men. It went something like this:

> "They buy you dinner, open your door, other than that, what are they good for? Men. They want a girl like the girl that married dear old Dad. That makes me so mad. Talking about men. Well, you can't beat 'em up 'cause they're bigger than you. You can't live with them and you just can't shoot them. Men, we're talking about men."

I have to admit, men do have problems with relationships. We grow up playing baseball, football, and basketball. A man thinks "talk" is a four-letter word. He thinks the relationship is going great if he doesn't have to talk. Putting him in a situation where he has to talk about relationships makes him very uncomfortable. That's why men go to the bathroom alone; that's the way God intended it.

Men have difficulty expressing themselves. When my daughters call, I say only three things, "How's the weather? Need any money? Here's your mother." A woman can talk on the phone for thirty minutes, and when you ask her who it was she says, "I don't know. They had the wrong number."

Men are simple. Women are complex. Women may even be smarter. Think about it. A woman's best friend is diamonds, and man's best friend is a dog.

I know women are more complex than men. When a woman is going out, she has to decide if she is going to wear her hair up or down, flats or high heels, slacks or a dress, casual or dressy dress, stockings, knee-highs or socks, jewelry or no jewelry, lots of make-up or a little make-up. A man picks up some clothes, smells them, and if there is no visible dirt he has himself an outfit. A man makes a fashion statement by turning the brim of his baseball cap backwards. Women dress to express themselves and men dress so they won't be naked.

I see things in one dimension. It works or it doesn't work. My wife sees it at a different level. For example, we moved into an almost new house with almost new wallpaper and Penny said, "That's got to go." I'm thinking, "Why? It's almost new, it covers the wall – it works." She says, "It's not me." I say, "It's not me either; it's wallpaper."

We have thirteen pillows on our bed. I ask myself, "Why? I have one head; I need only one pillow." The difference between men and women is best illustrated when you look at what women carry – a purse. It contains everything they might need. Men carry a wallet. It conveniently contains nothing but money, which means I can buy whatever I need. It's simple! Women, on the other hand, are complex. Actually, women have many purses. My wife has casual purses and formal purses, and she even has spring purses. Some women even buy a purse just to match their shoes. What would my friends do if I told them I couldn't wait for them to see my new spring wallet that matches my new shoes? They would run. Men are simple. Women are complex. These differences affect many aspects of a relationship.

When dealing with your wife, let me tell you what simply doesn't work, especially in the area of gifts. If your last gifts have been things like salad shooters, dust-busters, weed whackers, deluxe irons, and drywall compound, you are in serious trouble. They work, but they don't work with your wife. I was in serious trouble this year. I thought I did great. I got her a gift certificate. I still messed up; she said I got the wrong size.

Yes, men and women are different. That was God's plan. The difference is the dynamic. Together we are more than we ever could have been apart. That's why God said it wasn't good for man to be alone. He made him a helper to complete him...or was it to finish him off?

Home Alone

Life has different stages. Someone has said there are four stages of life: you believe in Santa Claus; you don't believe in Santa Claus; you are Santa Claus; and you look like Santa Claus. My wife and I are at the empty nest stage. That's kind of in between being Santa and looking like him. It took us about ten minutes to get used to this stage. I have raised three daughters (God doesn't send a son to a house where there's already a man), and survived pantyhose strangulation. I feel like the guy who went through seminary but never believed in original sin. About twenty years later he ran into one of his professors. The professor asked if he still didn't believe in original sin. He said that after raising teenagers and pastoring a church, he not only believed in original sin, but now he also believed in demon possession.

I'm now back to living with just my wife again, and she's gone to visit the girls. I'm home alone. I'm like most of you guys. I really out-punted my coverage when I married. Not only is my wife beautiful, but she's also organized. Everything has its place, and it better be there. She is thorough; she even proofreads a Xerox copy. That's probably why God brought her into my life. My life is random haphazardness. I have a photographic mind. I just lose the film. I try to get it together, but when I do I can't remember where I put it.

In clinical terms, Penny would be a compulsive neurotic. I would be what's clinically called sloppy. So God brought us together. Why? Because God likes to laugh, that's why.

Now, I have to admit Penny has gone overboard a few times. On vacation she used to want to clean up the car at every stop. I finally convinced her that's unrealistic, and we decided to follow my plan. Enjoy the trip and hose out the car when we get there. Sometimes she cleans up things even before I'm through with them – like the time I got up to go to the bathroom in the middle of the night and she made the bed. I have to admit, however, it has helped me – at least I'm faster. I read the paper in one sitting. If I ever put it down, it's gone.

Now, I'm home alone thinking about what life would have been like if I had remained single. Before I got married, I used to look in the refrigerator and play the "Unsolved Refrigerator Mystery" game. It's a great game. You find a friend and take ten things out of the refrigerator and guess what's under that green penicillin stuff and the one who loses has to eat it.

Well, the game is over and I lost, so I'm just sitting here in my chair looking around the house. I look around and see all the beautiful matching towels. We have regular towels that match the color scheme. Then we have guest towels that match the color scheme, but are just for guests. Then there are the "touch-me-not" towels that are for decoration only. And of course we have hand towels to accent the bigger towels that help bring out the appropriate color. If it were just me, I would have two towels – one wet and one dry. Alternate each day for about six months, then throw them away and get two more towels.

If I were single, I'd probably have one chair and one big TV and, of course, the remote control (appropriately named for all the dysfunctional males with MGMCTVD - Male Genetic Multi-Channel TV Disorder – who want to be remote but in control). When I look around, I see that Penny has put a lot of beauty in this place. No wonder God said it was not good for us to be alone. When God looked down He wanted to see something worth looking at – not two towels, a chair and a TV.

I read the other day that in the U.S., single men commit 80-90% of all crimes. So what do we do? We send them to prison with other men. What we should do is start a dating service. Find a good woman.

Well, got to go. The phone is ringing. It's Penny! "You're coming tomorrow?" Man, I've got to get this mess cleaned up quick. Where's that water hose?

Get the Connection?

My wife and I periodically take a personality inventory in which one can score either as a thinker or as a feeler. It shows whether you make decisions with your head or your heart. Thinkers and feelers gravitate to different kinds of occupations. A pastor, a doctor, and an engineer were waiting one morning for a particularly slow group of golfers. The engineer asked, "What's with these guys? We've been waiting for fifteen minutes." The doctor agreed, "I don't know, but this is ridiculous." The pastor noted, "Hey, here comes the groundskeeper. Let's have a word with him." The pastor called out to the groundskeeper, "Say, George, what's with the group ahead of us?" George said, "They are rather slow, aren't they? That's a group of blind firefighters. They lost their sight saving our clubhouse from a fire last year, so we always let them play for free anytime." The group was silent for a moment. The pastor sympathized, "That's so sad. I think I'll say a special prayer for them tonight." The doctor added, "That's a good idea. In fact, I'm going to contact my ophthalmologist buddy and see if there is anything we can do for these guys." The engineer suggested, "Well, in the meantime, why can't these guys play at night?" I think you know what category the engineer fell into.

The majority of men score in the thinking category while the majority of women score in the feeling category. In my marriage, it's just the opposite. I don't know if I think like a woman or Penny feels like a man. But it affects our relationship. The first time I was sick, I wanted some serious comfort. I wanted sympathy, understanding, breakfast in bed with Snickers and ice cream, and a little bit of encouragement. She said, "You're not that sick. Take a shower and go to work. You'll feel better later." Once I woke up with a backache, moaning and looking for some comfort. Penny said, "Get on the floor and do the exercises you are supposed to be doing. You'll feel better." I felt like the man who had a critical heart problem. The doctor called his wife in by herself and said, "Your husband is in bad shape. He will die unless you cook healthy foods for him, rub his neck, and meet his every need so that he can relax and not worry about anything." When they were alone her husband asked what the doctor had said. The wife replied, "He said that you're going to die."

Thinkers are like that. They don't gift-wrap things. One fellow that had one too many was stumbling home through a cemetery late one frosty night. He fell into an open grave. Pretty soon another inebriated type came along and heard the first fellow yelling from the hole in the ground, "Help. I'm cold. I'm cold." The second fellow peered into the open grave and said, "Well, no wonder. You kicked all your dirt off."

Inebriated thinkers are still thinkers. They have the ability to depersonalize things. Their humor is even different. They like jokes like the one about the war camp. The prison camp leader said, "Well, there's good news and there's bad news. First the good news: There is a change of underwear in the shower for everyone. But now the bad news: Smith you change with Jones, Jones you change with Smith..." You get the idea. If you are a thinker you are probably laughing. If you are a feeler, you are saying, "Yuck! How could he say that?"

I knew an administrator who was a thinker. People said he would fire his own mother. He replied, "No. I would never have hired her in the first place." Thinkers would rather be right than be liked. They don't worry about presentation; they just give you the cold, hard facts. Feelers gift-wrap everything.

Being liked is important to feelers. They are concerned with people's feelings; they understand people and want to help. Unfortunately, this means they have a tough time saying no. They are the ones at the family reunion trying to keep everyone happy, especially after some thinker just insulted everyone at the table.

So why do feelers get into trouble? Because in trying to take care of the whole world, they end up resenting the world. Feelers have to remember what you learn on the airplane. In times of trouble, first put the oxygen mask over your own face and then help your children. You can't take care of others if you don't first take care of yourself.

How should I make decisions? With my heart or with my head? Use both. Don't you know that they are connected? God connected them with a word. The word is love. Speak the truth in love. A gentle heart and a firm mind can get along when connected by love. Love connects a lot of opposites. It's kept my wife and me connected for a long time. She has even softened up to my sick spells. As a matter of fact she goes overboard. When she says, "Does my little boy have a runny nose?" It takes a little joy out of my ice cream. But her heart is right. And for a thinker, that's progress. So I respond, "Yes," and I also add, "Your little boy has a headache, too, which a Snickers would really help." So when heart and head are in competition, remember the love connection.

Get the Details: Primary Communication 101

What do women want to know? Everything! My parents usually call on Saturday and talk for about twenty minutes. Penny always asks, "What did they say?" I say, "Uh, uh, they said...they are coming in April." Penny says, "You talked twenty minutes, surely they said more than that." "Well, they sure did. They said, uh..." I can't think of another thing. I tell her, "It was just insignificant stuff, small stuff. It didn't matter, I can't even remember." She'll give me a look and say, "Okay." Then the next day, somebody brings up something that my dad had talked about on the phone and it reminds me of what he said. So I'm in a group of people and I say, "Oh yeah, my dad said..." and launch into a story. Penny gives me a look. After the story she grabs my arm and says, "See, you tell the whole world everything and you tell your wife nothing, *nothing, nothing.*" That happens regularly.

I'm a man, so I decided to fix this problem. *I'd had enough, and I was going to straighten out the situation.* The next time my parents called, I wrote down everything they said, even every little insignificant thing. That way, when Penny asked what they said I'd be able to recite everything. I thought this would finally put her in her place. The next time my parents called, Penny and the girls were at the mall. (The mall has it all. One day I expect them to come home with the escalator just because it was marked "down.") As we talked, I wrote down everything. The dog got into the tomatoes, the air conditioning bill was $235, everything. Then I just put it under my chair and waited for Penny to come home. When she came in, I didn't say anything. I just waited. (You have to know when to hold them and when to fold them.) Finally Penny said, "Did your parents call today?" "Yes, they did." "What did they say?" "Would you like to know everything they said?" "I'd like to know *anything* they said." "I'll tell you everything." I pulled out the paper and went through everything. The dog got into the tomatoes, the air conditioning bill, etc. I thought I had her good and she would never ask anymore. Finally, I got to the end, "They said goodbye and I said goodbye." Penny was happy. She was smiling. Now she wants me to take notes every time my parents call.

You see, men don't understand that women want details. But men aren't into details. Penny and I visited a couple and on the way home Penny said, "Did you like that dress she had on?" "You talking to me?" *(Most of the time, men bluff.)* "Yeah, I liked the dress." *(But they always catch you.)* "I didn't think you liked that color of green." "Oh, it was green? Well I guess I didn't like it." "You don't even know what I'm talking about, do you?" "No. I don't even remember she had on a dress." "Did you like the curtains in the family room?" "Which was the family room?" "Did you like the tile on the floor in the kitchen?" I'm thinking, "I don't have a clue." "Did you like the taupe color in the living room?" "Taupe color?" I didn't know there was a color called taupe. It's not in my paint by color set. Is this an imported color or something? Does God know about this color? Men just don't notice those things, and what we do notice we forget. That's why there is instant replay for men; they have already forgotten. I don't pay attention to the details. I can watch a rerun of *Murder She Wrote* and still not know who did it. We have to learn to pay attention because women want details.

Meeting the needs of a woman requires work. Typically a man will come home from work and his wife will say, "What happened today?" And he'll say, "Nothing." "Nothing? You were there from nine to six and nothing happened? Boy, they sure pay you pretty good for nothing." Men cannot think of anything that happened at work. But a woman wants to know these things. When I did marriage counseling, I advised the men to write the details of what happened that day at work on a 3x5 card.

One time, a co-worker of mine was expecting a baby. I told my secretary, "Penny wants to know when Laurie has her baby, so let me know when the baby is born." One day my secretary said, "Laurie had her baby; don't forget to tell Penny." I was excited because I could tell Penny something that happened. As usual, Penny said, "What happened at work today?" "Laurie had her baby." "What did she have?" "She had a baby." "They come in two kinds – boys and girls. What did she have?" "I don't know; I didn't ask." But I'm a good husband so the next day I asked my secretary what Laurie had. Then I told Penny, "Laurie had a boy." She said, "What did they name it?" "They named it a boy's name." The following day I told Penny, "Laurie named the baby Billy." She said, "How much did Billy weigh?" "Billy was a fat baby." You get the idea. Free advice: if someone has a baby at work, find out all the details. It's not enough to know that she had a baby.

To a woman intimacy means "into-me-you-see." So, guys, you have to talk to her. Tell her your hopes, fears, and dreams. At least tell her where you went for lunch today. And, ladies, keep it simple please. Stick to primary colors.

Fidget While You Talk

Relationships can be tough. This week I was exasperated with Penny and said, "I was a fool when I married you." She said, "Yes, dear, but I was too in love to notice." I think sometimes that if Penny really loved me she would have married someone else. We've had our share of conflicts. We made a commitment when we were married that we would never go to bed angry, so we stayed up all night every night the first three months of our marriage.

Most of our conflicts involve communication. Unfortunately, the early part of my life was spent as a boy. Boys grow up fidgeting instead of talking. They are activity oriented. We grew up playing King of the Hill and Capture the Flag. We put on a helmet and knocked someone down. Men think a relationship is going great when they don't have to talk.

Men like a no-huddle offense, all action. Women think a relationship is going great when the men in their lives have time to talk. Every night they seem to enjoy the huddle. Let's be honest. Most women talk about general things. Women can just sit and talk. That's very difficult for a man to do. He talks best when he's spraying WD-40 or hammering. Men talk better when they fidget. Guys just have to fidget. That's part of being a guy. Guys really never grow up. A five-year-old girl was crying. Her dad asked, "What's the matter?" She said, "I just learned that I have to grow up, and I can't be a little girl anymore." He pulled her close and said, "Honey, let me tell you a secret. You have to grow up on the outside but not on the inside. I'm still a little boy inside, but don't tell your mother." She wiped her tears and smiled up at her dad and said, "I think she already knows." Most wives know that guys never really grow up. Even when they grow up on the outside, they still play games like softball. That's a legitimate fidget for older, graying guys. They just can't seem to stop. Even when they hurt and ache and have to see the fidget doctors, the chiropractors, and the orthopedic surgeons, they can't keep from fidgeting.

I was talking to a friend of mine. He had just bought a brand new Buick. It was loaded and had a remote control that opened everything. It turned on the lights, locked and unlocked the doors, opened the trunk, and turned on the alarm. It did everything with just the push of a button. He and his wife decided to take a trip in their new car, and she had all of her hanging clothes laid in the trunk so they wouldn't wrinkle. They were neatly spread out. They stopped to get gas, and, with a full tank of gas, they got a free car wash. While in the car wash, my friend was killing time and decided to look at his remote. Men are men, and they like toys and gadgets and stuff, so he started to fidget with his new remote. He hit the wrong button and his trunk opened. Water and soap filled the trunk and washed his wife's clothes along with the car. Two hundred miles down the road he finally got up enough courage to say something. He said, "Honey, do you see the humor in this yet?" She said, "No."

Women don't understand fidgeting like men do. Women understand talking and men don't. Penny and I are working on a solution to this problem. She didn't want to divorce me just because I was a man, and we are committed to growing old and breaking our hips together. That is, unless she doesn't wring my neck first. I think we have found the answer to our problem. I love to play golf. God must have invented the game for men. I can fidget with a big stick, lots of them in fact, and I can hit something really hard. What a game! People ask me why I play golf. One reason is it is cheaper than Prozac. Another reason is that I can fidget. The golf swing lasts only about two seconds, so even if I hit the ball 100 times I've played golf for only 200 seconds. But it takes about four hours to play a round of golf. So what am I doing the other 14,200 seconds? I am riding around in a golf cart, drinking diet coke, and talking. That's how men talk. We fidget, talk, fidget, talk, fidget, talk, fidget and talk. Men can't just sit and talk. We have to have a little fidget while we talk. Penny has now taken up golf. One reason is so that she can talk to me. It's great. We fidget, talk, fidget, talk, fidget and talk.

Now that we have solved our communication problem we have another problem – competition. Men like to win. I think Penny understands that. Yesterday she made a putt that beat me on a hole, and the minute it went in she said, "Oops!"

Cornbread and Buttermilk

My wife and I are from different backgrounds. Her father is from up north, and my family came from way down south. Also, Penny grew up wealthy, and I grew up poor. Her swimming pool wasn't heated, but it was a different world. She had four baths, and I had four paths. One year our bathroom caught on fire, and we were excited because it didn't reach the house.

These differences affected our relationship even in what we ate. I didn't know what I was eating the first few years of marriage, but men will eat most anything. I got nostalgic for my childhood and the foods I ate when I was growing up. I started thinking about cornbread. I wanted cornbread. A man's ego is very big and he has a hard time sharing his needs. If I asked, "Honey, would you make me cornbread?" she might say, "no". Men don't handle rejection well, so I did what most men do. I dropped subtle hints.

We'd go to the grocery store, and I'd hang around the cornbread. I was sure that when Penny found me she'd know I wanted cornbread. But she didn't know what I was thinking, and finding me she'd ask, "What are you doing?" I'd say, "I'm looking at cornbread." She would just walk on by. I'd then say, "My goodness, look, Aunt Jemima Cornbread. She makes the best." She had no respect for Aunt Jemima. I'm thinking I want cornbread! When a cornbread commercial came on the TV, I'd say, "Look, Honey, that's cornbread," which she ignored. Finally after about five or six years, I knew the only way to get cornbread was to ask for it.

One day I had one too many Diet Cokes and was a little carbonated, so I got up the courage to say, "Penny, would you make me some cornbread?" She said, "Sure." That ticked me off because I had waited so long. Then she asked something that scared me. "What is cornbread?" I thought, "I'm in serious trouble here." She did get my mother's recipe and made it that day.

She met me at the door with a blindfold. Women do things differently. There are two ways to handle women, but nobody knows either one of them. They like surprises, celebrations, and candlelight. We had candlelight one night and I said, "Honey, what's the big occasion?" It was the grand opening of the grocery store. She led me to the table blindfolded. "Okay, take the blindfold off." I ripped that thing off, and I saw the cornbread. I said, "Honey, something's wrong with the cornbread, you killed it. It's got red stuff all over it; it's bleeding. What happened to the cornbread?" She said, "Well, I knew you loved strawberry jam, so I put half a jar of strawberry jam all over your cornbread." I said, "Oh, Honey, no. You ruined the cornbread." Then I said, "You did make the cornbread. Next time don't touch the cornbread. I need to show you how to eat cornbread."

About a week later she called and said, "I'm going to make cornbread." I said, "Don't touch it after you make it. I'm going to the store and pick up a few things. I'll show you how to eat cornbread tonight." I got buttermilk and green onions on the way home. I got my big glass, and she said, "I have a glass of tea for you." I said, "Be cool." I put that big glass down and started pouring the buttermilk. She said, "Honey, if I've told you once, I've told you a thousand times, when you buy milk, look at the date. That milk has curdled, it's spoiled, and it's no good." And I said, "Honey, that's *buttermilk*." She said, "I don't care who makes it; it's no good. Look at the date before you buy it." I just kept pouring buttermilk and grabbed my cornbread and attacked it. I put the cornbread into the buttermilk. Penny put her hands over my daughter's eyes (she was about three) and said, "Don't you look at your daddy. Don't you look at your daddy." I took a little bite of green onion and I took a bite of that cornbread and buttermilk, and she said, "I'm nauseated; I have to go." She left, but it was one of the best nights of my life. We've made a lot of progress since then. She can watch me eat buttermilk and cornbread without getting sick. If I had not communicated with her, I'd still be mad about cornbread. If you want something, you have to ask for it. And you, too, might have one of the best nights of your life.

Conflicting Ways

Been to battle lately? Conflict can actually be good for you. Criticism separates people, but conflict stimulates people. If you ignore things, they build up and get worse. You might as well fight the battle before you have to go to war.

A little boy asked his dad, "How did the war start?" "Which war?" asked his father. "The big war, how did it start?" "Well, it started when Germany invaded Belgium." His wife interrupted, "That isn't how the war started. It started when Germany invaded Poland." He argued, "That's not right; it was Belgium. I know my history." She said, "You don't know history. I'm the one who got you through college." He said, "You couldn't get me through anything; you've never been right about anything in your life." They continued to argue back and forth as the boy watched. Finally his father looked at his son and said, "What was your question again?" The little boy said, "Never mind. I know how wars start. They start small but then build up."

How do little battles lead to a big war? There are different strategies. The first is *My Way*. This is the most popular. "I am right. Do you agree with me, or are you wrong?" It's like the lady who prayed at breakfast, "Please make my husband be right today because you know he will never change his mind." This is the attitude of someone who is always right and must always win. Generally that battle has a winner and a loser.

People often use intimidation instead of negotiation. Their strategy is based on how they won in the past. This method is extremely attractive to males. Men like sports in which the object is to seriously injure the opponent. When you've won, you tend to use the strategy over and over.

Some women win by crying. If they don't win, then they cry and cry again. Men buy things; if they don't win, they'll buy, buy again. These methods are inappropriate and neurotic, but they work. People use whatever works for them, whether or not it's right or wrong.

When Penny and I were first married and we had an argument, I would pretend that I was a lawyer. I had exhibit A and exhibit B. Then I made one big point and looked at Penny and said, "The defense rests." She looked at me and asked, "Do you know what Capital Punishment is?" I might have won the battle, but I was definitely headed for war.

One strategy for solving conflict is *Your Way*. At times it is appropriate just to acquiesce to the other person. Some things are not as important to you as they are to your mate. When we moved to Texas, I really wasn't that concerned with the style of house and what the kitchen looked like. The only thing I wanted was a "split bedroom" model. The master bed and bath were on one end of the house, and the other bedrooms and bathrooms were on the other end. I knew I wanted my girls to be in their bathroom and not in mine. That's all I cared about and I could yield on everything else such as wallpaper, kitchen, and so forth. It just wasn't that important.

In a relationship, if you yield, you have to yield with a positive attitude. Some people yield, but do so with gritted teeth. One lady said that living with her family was like living in a foreign mission field, suffering for Jesus. "I give in. I give in. I'm a martyr." You don't need to be a martyr or a doormat. You don't need to be Edith from *All in the Family* – the classic doormat. In one scene a friend tells Edith, "Of all the people I know, you're the only one who has a happy marriage." Edith responds, "Really? Archie and me? Thank you." "What is your secret?" her friend asks. Edith says, "Oh, I don't have a secret. Archie and me still have our fights. Of course we don't let them go on too long. Somebody always says 'I'm sorry,' and Archie always says, 'It's okay, Edith.'" God put you together so that you can become more than you were when you were apart. At times you'll need to speak up and at other times give up when something is not as important to you as it is to your spouse.

Another way to solve conflict is *Half Way*. This is the way most people try to deal with conflict. I give a little, you give a little, and we compromise. The solution is often quicker, but the conflict is sometimes still unresolved.

The last strategy for handling conflict is the *Best Way*. Make a "we" decision. Decide that together you can make better decisions than you can apart. That means Penny and I decide that we're going to pray about any problem or decision and talk about it until we both agree on a solution. It may take a little longer, but it's the smartest thing to do. If I had included Penny in all of my decisions, many things would have worked out better. God puts people together so that we will have another way of looking at things. The "we" decision becomes a good decision and a God decision because you're getting input from both individuals. Some men don't profit from this because of ego and pride. I ran across a bumper sticker that illustrated this attitude: "If at first you don't succeed, do it the way your wife told you to."

One soldier told Abe Lincoln during the war, "We need to pray that God will be on our side." Lincoln said, "We had better pray that we are on God's side." God doesn't change sides. So if you're in a duel and you'd like it to be a duet, consider making it a trio. Get on God's side and discover that God's way is the best way.

Baby Talk

The first time I saw our oldest daughter, I saw a baldhead and heard powerful lungs. She was a loud noise at one end and no responsibility at the other. It was scary. Now I know why they say, "Hold the head." It's the safest part. I knew this baby was going to change my life when I asked my mother-in-law to stay over a few extra days just to help us. I didn't know what to do with my new daughter. By the end of the first day, I was so completely helpless, that I just took her to my mother-in-law. "Here's your problem," she said. "This baby's in serious need of a diaper change." Looking baffled, I said, "But the package says it's good for eight to ten pounds!"

Angela had colic so she woke up and cried almost every night. Now what do two mature people, one being a psychologist, do when the baby cries at night? First of all, we would both lie there as long as we could, pretending to be more asleep than the other. She was thinking, "If he were a good husband, he'd get up." And I was thinking, "If she were a good wife, she'd get up." So we played that game for a while until we finally had to do something. Obviously, Angela wasn't just crying, by now she was screaming. Then Penny, because she's more mature, said something like, "Do I hear Angela crying?" That didn't mean, "Do I hear Angela crying?" She knew she was crying. That really meant, "Get up and see about Angela." I knew what she meant but resented her telling me. She reminded me that the night before I had said, "I'll get it the next time." I said, "I didn't mean the next time the baby cried; I meant the next baby." So we fought over who was going to take care of Angela while she was still crying. We had to learn to communicate.

We had to learn to communicate about Angela, and then we had two more daughters, so we had to get a plan. For the first two, I would get the baby and bring her to Penny. She would change her while I went downstairs to heat the bottle. Then I would bring the bottle to Penny. She would feed her and when she was asleep, I would put her back into the bed. That was a great plan, but Penny nursed our last child so I didn't have to mess with the bottle. I just had to get the baby. Then we decided since Saturday was the only day we could sleep, we would take turns sleeping in on alternate Saturdays. Of course we had a few misunderstandings about who had slept in the previous Saturday. Since men have amnesia when it comes to remembering anything that doesn't involve athletic statistics, and Penny can remember not only what time she got up last Saturday but what outfit she was wearing, I think I put in a few more Saturdays than I had coming to me. The bottom line is, we decided to work it out instead of have it out. We decided to talk about it instead of fight about it.

Why is communication so difficult? Consider this: When you were a baby, you had needs that you couldn't articulate so you didn't communicate in a positive way. You didn't say to yourself, "I'm hungry. I'm going to smile when mother comes by and maybe she'll know I'm hungry and feed me." Likewise, you couldn't tell your mother that your diaper needed to be changed. So, when you had a need, you just screamed, and the louder you screamed the quicker she came. You learned that when your needs weren't met or when you were frustrated, you could act bad, and the worse you acted, the quicker people met your needs.

The same thing happens in marriage. When you are frustrated you provoke the people around you as much as you can so they will meet your needs. You sulk, pout, make cutting remarks, and think that surely someone will come and meet your needs. That's how infants behave. Let me give you a little rhyme. Before you have a baby in a carriage, you'd better deal with the baby in your marriage. Why? Because two babies married to each other – and then having a baby – make one big mess.

Stages of Marriage

The first stage of a relationship is that wonderful stage, the urge to merge. You're in hormone heaven. You've found the perfect person. She always looks good, smells good, and never goes to the bathroom. Then you get married, and another stage begins. It's war. Before marriage, opposites attract. If you have a Dead Sea personality, you are attracted to a babbling brook. After marriage, opposites attack. The very thing that attracted you now ticks you off. Sometimes it starts early. One couple got up on the first day after their honeymoon and he said, "Where's my hot breakfast? Mother always made me a hot breakfast." She responded, "If you want a hot breakfast, stick your Fruit Loops into the microwave." And the war has started. You realize you don't have a perfect person. He doesn't always look good, smell good, and sometimes he spends a lot of time in the bathroom.

I married what I affectionately call the original Mrs. Clean. Everything has its place and it better be there. I knew I was in trouble when Penny wanted to clean up the rice at the wedding before we left on our honeymoon. In her closet, all the clothes are color-coded, and the shoes face north. This girl is precise. For her, cleanliness is next to godliness.

For me, if cleanliness is next to godliness, I must be an atheist. I'm what is clinically called sloppy. I thought God made poster beds for pants, shirts, and underwear. I think it was my underwear on her side of the bed that really ticked her off. You might say we had a brief problem.

It was an adjustment. I had to read the paper in one sitting or it would be thrown away. I had to keep an eye on my Diet Coke glass or it would be in the dishwasher. I asked her one day, "What do you think God is teaching me by giving me a wife who cleans things up before I'm finished?" She said that God was trying to teach me to enjoy things while I had them because I never knew when I was going to lose them. The war stage was tough.

Unfortunately, most people continue the war. One time the Devil visited the church, and everybody ran out of the building except for one man on the second row. He didn't move and just sat there. The Devil said, "Do you know who I am?" He said, "Yes." The Devil said, "Are you afraid of me?" He said, "No, not a bit." The Devil said, "You know who I am, and you're still not afraid? Why not?" The man said, "I've been married to your sister for fifty-three years." Now that's a guy who stayed in the war.

A lady went to a gun shop to buy a revolver for her husband. The salesman asked, "Did your husband mention any model that he liked?" She said, "No. He doesn't know I'm going to shoot him yet." It's a verbal war.

It's hard to let go of the "perfect person fantasy." We get discouraged when Cinderella turns into a nag, and Prince Charming turns into a toad. The fact is, there are no perfect people, and the reason you didn't get someone any better is because of your own imperfections. The way to end the war is to tear up the fantasy picture of a perfect person and accept the real person as a gift from God. You need to realize that the very things that irritate you are the areas that you need to work on and grow in. If you don't tear up the picture, you'll spend your life tearing up the person by trying to make her look like your fantasy. Oh, you'll sleep with the enemy and kiss her every now and then, but it will still be war.

The third stage of marriage is work. You decide that incompatibility is why you got married, and that together you can be much better than you could have been apart. In my marriage, I've learned to become self-disciplined and hang up my britches, and Penny has loosened up to the point that she lets me enjoy the entire Diet Coke before it goes into the dishwasher.

The best way to continue the work of marriage is to understand the worship of marriage. Realize that people need love the most when they least deserve it. And you don't love them because of what they do but because of who you are: a person who is loved with a perfect love. Until you realize that you are loved with a perfect love, you cannot love imperfect people. When perfect love casts out all of your fear, you learn to worship the ground your spouse walks on, which takes you back to the wonderful stage. That, and separate bathrooms, will make a wonderful marriage.

Wedding Wake-Up Call

Relationships are confusing these days. I read that there is a rock star's son who plans on marrying his ex-wife's mother. His son from a previous marriage announced his engagement to the mother of the rock star's former wife. The marriage will make the rock star his ex-wife's step-grandfather. I think.

People marry again and again. A pastor's phone rang on Tuesday morning. It was a call from a young woman who didn't identify herself. She stated that she wanted to be married on Friday of that week. This was to be her sixth marriage. Not wanting to sound rude, the pastor said that he did not do spur-of-the-moment weddings. He told her he liked to counsel with the couple before the wedding. She sounded somewhat irritated by his response. After a pause, she continued, "Well, I'll find someone else to perform the ceremony, but I want you to know that I believe you are wrong about spur-of-the-moment weddings. Some of my best marriages have been spur-of-the-moment."

People marry so many times that we now play the Married Name Game. For example, If Sandra Locke married Elliott Ness, then divorced him to marry Herman Munster, she would be Sandra Locke Ness Munster. If Liv Ullman married Judge Lance Ito, then divorced him and married Jerry Mathers, she'd be Liv Ito Beaver. If Snoop Doggy Dog married Winnie the Pooh, he would be Snoop Doggy Dog Pooh. Well, you get the idea. That reminds me of another merger between Fed Ex and UPS. They would be called Fed Up.

It's not easy being a person of the cloth these days. I knew one minister whose wedding ceremony consisted of, "Do you whoever-she-or-he-may-be take this person as your lawful wedded whatever-it-is-you're-planning-to-call-it?"

The whole wedding scene seems so fake, even the announcement. The groom could be the worst guy in the world, yet he sounds like a cross between Billy Graham and the pope. For once I'd like to hear the truth, a wedding announcement that reads something like this: The groom is a popular young jerk who hasn't done an ounce of work since he got kicked out of college. He has nice clothes and keeps a supply of money because his dad is a softhearted old fool who covers his bad checks instead of letting him go to jail where he belongs.

We lose touch with reality. As a psychologist I've done my share of premarital counseling. It is an exercise in futility. The bride says, "The groom drinks a lot now, but he's going to quit when we get married." Or, "He doesn't go to church now, but he will after the ceremony." I want to say, "Do you know what a hundred to one odds are?" I ask a few questions like, "Where are you going to live?" They don't know. "Have you finished your education?" They haven't. "Do you have a job?" They don't. "What are you going to live on?" They shrug. Then they look at each other with goo-goo eyes and answer, "Love." They have the urge to merge and can't keep their hands off each other. One gland is calling out after another gland, and they are in hormone heaven. The chemistry is there but reality isn't. I want to say, "I give you five years for this body chemistry to turn to toxic waste." I'm nice, though, and suggest that maybe they should register paper plates instead of china. I do add that they should probably register at Toys "R" Us, because they don't have a clue.

Ceremonies are also getting more and more expensive and elaborate. I really don't want to see pictures of the bride and groom from their engagement or a video that would rival Hollywood. I want to say to the groom, "Wipe that silly grin off your face because you have no idea what is happening. You can't play this marriage video in reverse and walk out of this thing later on. This is real." I know the father of the bride isn't smiling – he's paying for this extravaganza. At Christmas he's going to be singing, "Hock, the Herald Angels Sing."

When the couple asks how much they owe the pastor for performing the ceremony, he should say, "I'll take 10% of what you just blew in the last forty-five minutes." But most are kind and say, "Just pay me according to your bride's beauty." That works. As a matter of fact, one guy gave the pastor $200. I was shocked. I lifted the veil, took a look, and told the pastor to give $100 back. Just kidding.

One pastor said he would rather perform funerals than weddings. They pay more and last longer. He said the first person saved under his preaching is a backslider, the first couple he married is divorced, but the first person he buried is still there.

Maybe a wedding is a funeral in which you smell your own flowers. Or maybe a funeral is really a wedding when you "wake up" and find out what true love is.

2

Balancing Act

We're going too fast. We have to make this life last. I need this chapter. I knew I needed it when I read a book entitled *A Year's Worth of Meditation to Slow You Down* in four days. Are you constantly in a hurry, yet tired at the same time? Are you overwhelmed by life and always a week away from being caught up? If you have no time to read this chapter, then guess what: I wrote it for you. Actually, I wrote it for me, but I don't have time to read it right now.

Are We in a Hurry Again?

I can drive, but I get places so much faster on a plane. My finances are on Quicken, so I know instantly that I have enough money to fly. This morning I started my day with Nestlé Quik hot chocolate, and later I began my diet with Slim Fast, but then I stopped for some fast food. I dropped off some pictures at Fast Photo, my car at Ten Minute Lube, my laundry at One Hour Cleaners and got to the airport only to realize I had forgotten my notes, so I pulled out my Sprint Card and told my secretary to Fed Ex the material to my hotel. I parked in Fast Park and grabbed the Rapid Shuttle. I hurried to get on the plane so I could carry my baggage and not have to wait at baggage claim. Then I caught the Quick Shuttle to my hotel. I went to Express Check-in and had just enough time to go for a quick swim, but I couldn't find my Speedo swimsuit so I decided to work. I listened to a tape on fast speed. The speaker sounds a little like Donald Duck. I listened to an hour-long seminar in forty-five minutes. That's fast.

I remember that back when I had young kids, life wasn't so fast. Kids will slow you down, especially when they're in the concrete stage of development when they see, touch, smell, or lick everything they come into contact with. I saw a boy with a burned lip and asked how he burned it. He said, "I licked my nightlight." I asked, "Why?" He said, "I'd never licked one before." Kids slow us down because they don't want to miss anything.

Our girls loved Oreos. They ate the top layer off two cookies and then put them together to double the cream. Then they ate it very slowly because they wanted the good part to last as long as possible. I think that's why God gave us kids: to slow us down so we can make the best part last as long as possible. God has His own way of slowing us down. He put bones in fish, seeds in watermelon, and that little pain in the side of your head when you eat ice cream too fast.

I can remember when one of my kids earned a surprise. I had promised to take her to the store, so we stopped by a quick shop to get her surprise. I guess I was a little too restless because she turned to me and said, "Daddy, are we In a hurry again?" I realized she probably thought her name was Hurry instead of Kasey because I was always telling her to hurry. So this time I said, "No, Kasey, we are not in a hurry. Take as much time as you want to pick out your surprise." And she did. I think she touched, picked up, and cuddled everything in the store.

As I look back, seeing her make one of her first choices in life is one of my best memories. When we got to the car, she said it would be okay if I listened to one of those Donald Duck tapes. Even then I was listening to sermons on fast speed. I asked if she were sure and she said, "I don't understand sermons anyway so making them sound like Donald Duck makes it fun." It was a great lesson for me. Most people don't understand sermons anyway. Maybe I should spend more time *with* people than preaching *to* them.

The girls are grown now, and I'm off to speak, and I'm in the fast lane again. But God knows how to slow me down – He's given me grandkids. I'm even thinking about licking a nightlight. I've never done that before. Actually, I think I'll settle for the double cream Oreos. However, I bet it will be hard to eat slowly.

Small Things Mean A Lot

Several years ago Penny and I went to Hawaii. It was a great trip except for the day we went snorkeling. My wife loves the water. She grew up with a swimming pool in the backyard. I grew up a little differently; the bathroom was in our backyard. The only water I ever saw was Saturday night bath time. Consequently, I didn't learn to swim well until I met Penny. She's like a graceful fish in water; I'm more like a beached whale.

But I love her, and she loves the water, so we planned a day of snorkeling.

Some friends of ours had lent us their snorkeling equipment. As we were getting ready, I noticed one little thing was missing from my equipment. I couldn't find the little rubber circle that Penny was fitting over her snorkeling tube. It wasn't there. It was lost; it had gone wherever my lost socks go. I thought, "What's the big deal? It's small; it can't do much." I'm ready. Let's go.

We went deeper and deeper, admiring the beautiful fish. I went a little deeper and inhaled half of the Pacific Ocean. I realized then that the small, round circle keeps your snorkeling tube from tipping into the water. I thought I was going to die. My life flashed before me. Actually, a lot of other people's lives flashed before me first. I've done so much counseling and heard so many problems it took a while for my life to flash. Penny came to my rescue and I survived, but I'll never forget the value of small things.

As I think about it, the way we handle the small things pretty much determines how successful we are. Just think about it. How many of you have ever been bitten by a lion or tiger, or stepped on by an elephant? Very few I imagine. On the other hand, how many have been stung by a bee, bitten by a mosquito, or harassed by a fly? If you've ever spent the night with a mosquito or fly, you know how powerful small things can be.

It is an interesting phenomenon to watch the little things become big things. As I'm writing, I'm sitting at a table in my study. It looks awful. Just one small thing at a time, a paper here, a book there, a Diet Coke can over there. No big things are on my table, but the table is a mess. Last week it was clean; of course, I was out of town, but it was clean. Life can become a mess if you neglect the small things. Even small, loose ends can tie you up.

On September 11, 1995, a squirrel climbed onto the Metro-North Railroad power lines near New York City. He set off an electrical surge which weakened an overhead bracket which let a wire dangle toward the tracks, which tangled in a train which tore down all the lines. As a result, 47,000 commuters were stuck in Manhattan for hours that evening. I'll bet it wasn't even a big squirrel.

An enormous pine tree growing in the mountains of Colorado was only half-grown when the Pilgrims landed at Plymouth Rock. A close study revealed that it had been struck by lightning fourteen times and survived centuries of Colorado's hard winters. Age didn't destroy it. Avalanches didn't move it. Fires didn't kill it. Many came to believe the old tree was indestructible. But, in the end, a beetle destroyed it. A little pine beetle, so small you could crush it between your thumb and finger, destroyed that large tree.

One reason small things are important is that they lead to big things. Addition comes before multiplication, crawling before walking, and high school before college. No one starts at the top except a gravedigger. If you want to do great things in your life, start doing small things in a great way.

If you want to have a great marriage, do the small things. You may say, "I would die for my wife." She doesn't want you to die for her; she just wants you to take out the trash. Whisper three small words in her ear like, "I love you," or better yet, "Let's eat out." Try giving her a small thing, like the remote control. See, I told you small things are powerful. Dinosaurs are extinct, yet rabbits abound.

Big things really do come in small packages. I'm a grandpa, and I know small things mean a lot, for I would give the world to help one of my grandchildren. Yes, small things are powerful. Maybe that is why God used a baby to change the world.

Down To Earth Advice

"To everything there is a season and a time for every purpose under the heaven." Does that phrase sound familiar? What you sow is what you reap, so if you plan to live on this planet with any sort of ease, you must follow the rules.

God set up an orderly world. "While the earth remains, planting and harvest, cold and heat, winter and summer, and day and night shall not cease." Sounds fairly simple doesn't it? Realize that life is seasonal. If you understand the principles of the seasons, you can apply these to your life.

In life, difficult times, or winter, come on a regular basis. There is winter in your marriage, job, health, economics, relationships, and just about every other aspect of life. If you haven't yet lived through a tough winter, get ready – you will. The best way to endure winter is to be prepared. But most importantly, remember that spring is coming. Good times will follow bad times, and, for having endured the bitter cold, you can enjoy the newness of life in the spring.

Spring is full of choices that affect the harvest in your life. In springtime, you plant what you will harvest in the fall. Hard work reaps a plentiful harvest, and it begins with carefully planning and planting the seeds of your life. Don't waste the springtime.

Remember four words for the summer: effort, enemies, evaluation, and endurance. Like spring, summer requires effort. You must be disciplined in your chores and responsibilities if the crops you planted in the spring are to survive the summer heat. Realize there are spiritual disciplines in your life. Apply them regularly, and you will be able to stand the heat.

If you have a garden or farm, weeds, bugs, and diseases will invade it. You have to love good and hate evil. If you don't hate the enemies, they will destroy your marriage, family, relationships, and everything good that God has for you. Recognize your enemies and be prepared to guard what is growing.

Summer is a time for evaluation. Understand where you have been and where you are going. This insight allows you to plan for the future. You must make the necessary changes before winter comes and it is too late.

Fall is a time for judgment. God made the seasons for you to know what is fair and just. You reap from what you plant, and much more. The miraculous and supernatural yield whirlwinds out of the wind, bushels out of a seed, trees out of a tiny seedling, fields of flowers from one rainfall, and celebration of life if you planted carefully.

Your Resignation Has Been Accepted

We get into lots of problems when we try to control the world. We also waste a lot of energy on things we can't control. You can devise a great strategy and even pray all night that the sun will not come up, but it will. When the north wind blows, you can say and do anything you want, but it's going to blow. The best thing to do is to find your heavy coat.

A nervous passenger once asked the captain of an ocean liner what would happen if the ship hit an iceberg. "Nothing," replied the captain. "The iceberg would move right along as if nothing happened." That's the way life is; it's going to move right along.

None of us controls the universe. Even if we did, how would we know what was good or what was bad? Even Garth Brooks understood that. He sang a song entitled "Thank God for Unanswered Prayers." I can identify with that. Do you remember being in high school or college and being in hormone heaven? You had to marry that particular person, but it just didn't work out. You were devastated and thought, "How can life go on?" Then many years later you saw the person and thought, "Thank God for unanswered prayers!"

Life is like a parade. We see only what is in front of us, but God sees the whole parade. He has a greater perspective than we have. My favorite football team hired a great coach and paid him millions of dollars. But if you watch him on the sidelines, he has a headset on and he's taking advice from an assistant coach who is up in the press box. Why? Because the coach knows that the other guy has a better perspective.

I often feel like that. Many times I don't understand what's going on down here. I need someone who looks at life from above. Let me explain it this way: A little boy had a toy boat that he played with at the pond. One day his boat drifted away from him, and he tried everything he could to get it back, but he couldn't reach it. All of a sudden, as he was watching the boat and trying to figure out what to do, he saw a man throwing rocks at the boat. The little boy turned around in anger and said, "What are you trying to do, sink my boat? What are you doing?" The man just smiled and kept throwing rocks. The little boy yelled, "Quit it!" Finally he ran to the man. "What are you doing?" The man replied, "I'm trying to help you." "What do you mean trying to help me? You're going to wreck my boat." The man said, "Look at your boat." As the boy looked at his boat, he realized that the man was throwing the rocks over his boat. The ripples of the water were bringing his boat back to the shore.

What's the bottom line? Resign. Resign as General Manager of planet Earth. With your hand over your heart, repeat these words: "I, being of sound mind, do fully realize and admit that I do not now, nor have I ever, nor will I ever, run planet Earth. Therefore, I hereby offer my resignation as General Manager of planet Earth."

Feel better already, don't you? Now that you've resigned, remember that rocks can create ripples, and that God sees the whole parade. Believe me, that makes the clowns of life's parade a whole lot funnier.

Enjoy the Leftovers

Is the pace of your life too fast? Does cleaning up your dining area mean throwing fast food bags out of the back of the van? Has your grocery list been on the refrigerator so long that some of the products don't exist any more? Do you drive through McDonald's and ask for your order to go? Do you forget your twin brother's birthday? Do you ask at the dollar store, "How much is this?" Are you stressed out?

Did you ever wonder why a pigeon walks so funny? A pigeon walks that way to see where it's going. A pigeon has difficulty focusing its eyes so it must bring its head to a complete stop before each step to refocus. It's time for us to stop and refocus. Don't just slow down; stop.

There is a difference between stopping and slowing down. A man was pulled over for running a stop sign. He argued to the officer that he had slowed down and looked both ways. The officer said, "You have to stop." They continued the discussion, the man insisting he had slowed down and the officer insisting that he had to stop. The man told the officer there was no difference between stopping and slowing down. With that remark, the officer said, "Get out of the car." The officer started to beat the man with a billy stick. "Sir," said the officer, "would you like for me to stop or just slow down?" The man finally understood the difference between stopping and slowing down – which in this case was about $110.

We need to stop to think about where life is headed and what kind of connections we are making. This is a sign of maturity.

I'm a grandpa now. You know what two-year-olds are like. They are immature. They don't say, "Papa, I'm getting cranky and irritable and I'm not sharing well. I need a nap." They've never said that to me. Yet I'm around adults to whom I want to say, "You're cranky, you're irritable, you're not sharing well. You need a nap."

The best way to enjoy some peace in life is to add some space. Space is the difference between your limit and your load, the place where you have a little left over. It's like having a little breath left after reaching the top of the stairs. Space is having a little money left over at the end of the month. Space is having a little time left over before the deadline. Space is having a little bit left over.

Do you remember the days of leftovers? I do. On Sundays we had a big meal, usually with roast beef. That night we had leftovers. I loved those roast beef sandwiches. I looked forward to the leftovers. A friend of mine said that he *always* had leftovers at his house – he never saw an original meal. Leftovers are nice. It means you have enough space in the pace of your life.

Let me personalize this. Space means you have enough time to read this article twice. Let me visualize it for you. Let's say you make plans to go to Florida for vacation. The travel agent books you a ticket to Florida with a layover in Atlanta. You arrive in Atlanta at 11:46 a.m. and you depart on the next plane at 11:48 a.m. You have a two-minute connection in Atlanta. What do you think? You think that you can make it if you sit at the front of the plane and carry on your baggage. Maybe you can be the first off the plane. Maybe your connecting flight will be late and this plane will be early. Maybe your plane will be parked next to your connecting flight. If things are perfect, this schedule just might work.

Most of us get up each day and think we can make that two-minute connection, hoping we can make it all work. Maybe things will happen just the way they need to happen so you can get through the day. Guess what? It never happens that way. There are no one-hour delays, only three-hour delays. Planes never connect in the same gate area. I've never been on a plane that arrived early when I needed to make a close connection. Life doesn't work that way.

A man was driving on the Tri-state freeway in Chicago. His hat blew off in the middle of busy traffic. He stopped the car, ran across the freeway to get his hat, and was hit and killed instantly. The man who wrote the article about the accident observed, "It's amazing that you can lose everything chasing nothing."

Stop. Don't just slow down, but stop. Think about the connections in life. Do we spend more time shopping for the people we love than spending time with them? Let's leave enough space to stop. Otherwise, the pace will squeeze the love, the life, and the laughter out of you. If you want to finish the race with grace, put a little space in your life. Enjoy the leftovers.

How Do You Spell Space?

When was the last time you had some space in your life? Space is having time to fix the roof before it rains. Space is having the car serviced before it breaks down in traffic. Space is raising teenagers and still having a little love left. In our society we don't have much left over any more. There isn't much space. If you don't believe me, look in your closet.

A pastor, when asked if he took Mondays off, replied, "No, I don't want to feel that bad on my own time." It sounds as if he needed some space. How do we add space to our lives? Let me spell it out for you.

First, you have to **STOP**. Take some time every day to think not only about *what* you're doing, but also *why* you're doing it. Don't just slow down. Stop. There is a difference.

Next, **PREPARE**. Prepare for the wrecks of life. Life takes funny bounces – like the preacher who prayed for a big church and a pretty wife. His prayer was almost answered. He got a pretty church and a big wife. Sometimes life hits you in the stomach. Prepare.

Harry Houdini performed many outrageous stunts. Houdini's success as America's greatest magician was because of his emphasis on preparation and timing. His metal-like fingers and iron-nerved personality made him appear invulnerable. One day, answering a dare, he allowed a boxer to hit him full force in the stomach. But his timing was a split second off, and the boxer's fist slammed into him before he was prepared. Houdini reeled but managed to regain his posture. "Not that way," he coughed, "I've got to get set. Now hit me." The boxer hit again, smashing his fist against a seemingly granite abdomen. Ten days later, the great Houdini died from the injury inflicted by the boxer's first blow. He had not been sufficiently prepared.

Even when things go wrong, planning ahead can help us pick up the pieces and keep moving forward. As golfer Tommy Bolt advised, "Always throw your clubs ahead of you; that way you don't have to waste energy going back to pick them up."

Next is **ATTITUDE**. Attitude is focusing on the good in a situation. It is establishing some space. Space is a big part of attitude. Why? Attitude means you are willing to make space before you decide a situation is bad. At first glance it looks bad, but given time (space) it may turn out to be good. Attitude is not fact but focus.

A vulture sees only rotting meat because that is all it looks for. It thrives on that diet. But the hummingbird ignores the carcasses and the smelly flesh of dead animals. Instead, it looks for the tiny blossoms of the cactus flowers. It buzzes around until it finds colorful blooms, even those that are hidden from view by rocks. Each bird finds what it is looking for, and so will you.

CONCENTRATION Discern what your gifts are and what they are not, and say yes only to the best and not just to everything others want you to do. Nothing is more tiring than doing a job you hate. Beethoven never cleaned his house. When it got dirtier than he could stand, he moved. I wouldn't go that far, but I would take another speaking engagement, which I love, to pay for someone else to work on a broken kitchen appliance, which I hate. They pay me, I pay him, I'm happy, he's happy, the economy is better; you get the idea.

Finally, you must **E**NGAGE in energy renewing activities which energize you rather than drain you. The difference between space and stress is the difference between your limit and your load. And if your load and limit are the same, you have to work on increasing your limit because sometimes you can't do much about the load. You have to increase your energy level to have space.

A young boy, whose father was engrossed in the sports page, stood next to his father's recliner. He impatiently pounded the leather of his baseball glove. Finally the energetic little guy said, "Play with me or trade me." Much of life is more draining than energizing. Learn what those situations are and know when it is time to say, "Play me or trade me." But don't forget that sometimes it is okay to sit on the bench.

A life without space will be like a race that goes faster and faster and has no end. The race can squeeze the love, life, and laughter out of you. But space can give you time to laugh, live, love, and even time to sit on the bench when you need to. So, to run your life with grace, just add a little more space. **S**top, **P**repare, **A**ttitude, **C**oncentrate, and **E**ngage.

Pause at the Top

A man watched the driver of a truck carrying a load of chickens stop every half mile, get out of the truck, beat the side with a baseball bat until the chickens were flying in the air, get back into the truck, and drive off. He watched this routine happen time after time, and finally he pulled up beside the man and said, "I can't stand it. I've been watching you for some time. Why do you pull over and beat the truck with a bat to make the chickens fly?" The man said, "Well, I have a big problem. I have a half-ton truck and a ton of chickens, so I have to keep about half of the chickens flying all the time." Have you ever felt like that?

Life is a rat race, and even the animal kingdom is affected. Three snails mugged a turtle. When the turtle was asked what the muggers looked like he said, "I don't know; it all happened so fast."

The theme of life today is "do more and do it faster." A restaurant promises lunch in fifteen minutes or it will be free. An emergency room promises treatment in twenty minutes or it will be free. Of course you can even die fast; just call Dr. Kevorkian. People are reading *The Fifty-nine Second Employee* – a book about how to stay ahead of *The One-Minute Manager*. We have e-mail, overnight delivery, beepers, pagers, voice-mail, and cell phones. You can't go anywhere you can't be found. One guy told me to send him a fax on his car phone-fax. Can we do that? Doesn't he have to pull over or something? Our world is into speed.

I'm trying to get organized. Experts tell me to handle a piece of mail only once. I'm afraid to touch anything. My computer doesn't understand me. I've named it the Bermuda Triangle. Stuff goes in, but it never really comes back out. It gives new meaning to the word "backup." I have so many emergencies that I've changed my area code to 911. I've discovered that when life is going 100 mph you can't control it; you can only aim it. I use the express lane for the altar call at church. Every time I turn around it is "do it faster" – push the envelope, raise the bar, take it to the next level. I feel like the juggler at the circus, but I'm juggling hand grenades instead of balls.

Everyone has this problem. I knew our society was in trouble when I saw a lady get on the plane and put a laptop in her lap and her child in the overhead-baggage compartment. I am going to slow down. I am going to relax. I'm actually going to relax better and faster. I'm taking relaxation to the next level. Sorry – I got carried away.

I'm tired of desktop dining and information hell. I don't want to be reached at www.doItfast.com. I've decided to take my mother's advice. If she has said it once, she has said it a thousand times, "Charles Shelby, be still." When she used my middle name, I knew it was important because she usually called me by my brothers' names, or even worse, my sister's. So I'm going to be still. The two most important buttons on my computer from now on are going to be *delete* and *off*. Of course, you can't simply turn off the computer; it asks if you are sure if you want to sign off. YES! I'm sure.

I'm not saying to drop everything. There is a season of accomplishment, but there is also a season of rest and there is a season of evaluation. Understand that five times zero is still zero. Some things are not worth doing even if you can do them five times faster. So I threw away my to-do list. Maybe if it's not important enough to remember, it may not be important enough to do. I turned off my computer and took a golf lesson.

My golf teacher said, "It's no wonder you don't have any power. Your back swing is too fast. I got whiplash just watching it. A pause at the top is what gives you the power." He was reflecting on what my mom had said, "Charles Shelby, be still." His emphasis was to be *still* at the top.

In the early days of aviation, a gutsy pilot accepted the challenge of flying around the world. One day, as he was drifting through the silent skies above the Atlantic Ocean, he heard an annoying sound in the electrical wiring. A rat had climbed aboard and was inflicting potential damage to the plane's electrical system with its razor sharp teeth. The pilot began to worry and anticipate his potential demise. Then he remembered that rats can live only in low altitudes. He flew his plane to the highest altitude that he and his plane could tolerate. He stayed at that altitude until the annoying sound stopped. Upon landing, he found a dead rat in his instrument panel.

The lesson is simple. Whether it is planes, golf, or life, take it to the top and pause. You will have more power, and all the ratty issues of life won't seem so important.

The Road Runner's Path – Beep, Beep

Have you noticed that movement and direction are two separate things? When you're lost in the parking lot and going in circles, you're still moving – you're just not getting anywhere. Why? Because no one ever invented a compass that points in a useful direction, like toward the place where you parked your car.

The key to success in life is not to shoot the bull, pass the buck, or make seven copies. It is finding and staying on the right path. How do you find the path that leads to the top? You need a plan.

I heard about a knight who came in to see his king after a great battle. He rode in on his limping horse, leaning to one side, bloody, bruised, and scarred with his armor dented and helmet skewed. The king said, "What hath befallen you, Sir Knight?" Straightening up as best he could, he replied, "Oh, sire, I have been laboring in your service, robbing and burning and pillaging your enemies to the west." "You've been what?!" cried the startled nobleman. "I haven't any enemies to the west!" "Oh!" There was a long pause, and the knight finally said, "Well, Sire, you do now." The moral to this story is enthusiasm is not enough. You need direction and a path.

Many people approach life with a "fire, ready, and aim" mentality. Aren't you glad that grocery stores have numbered aisles and a plan? Can you imagine the chaos if items were randomly placed? I have enough trouble when Penny sends me for peas and discover that there are seven different kinds of peas. Thank goodness they are all on the same path.

You have to plan, but you also have to practice your plan. Some people approach life with a "ready, aim, and aim" mentality. They never do anything. They are aiming to do this or aiming to do that, but they never actually pull the trigger. It's like a guy who buys building materials but never actually builds a house. When you ask him when he will start, he describes the building materials he's just ordered. He will always be one plank short of a building.

A path begins with the first step. You plan, practice, and then make progress. Where you are on the path is not as important as how far you've come. Life is like riding a bike; if you don't keep going forward, you'll fall off. We have to continue to make progress.

A man complained that he hurt his leg when he fell off a 50-foot ladder. His friend said, "You must be hurt badly." He said, "No, I was only on the second step." Progress means that other steps follow the first step.

Persistence means hanging in there. Worthwhile endeavors always come with struggles. There are no shortcuts to anyplace worth going. Sir

Edmund Hillary, the first man to conquer Mount Everest, said, "It's not about conquering mountains; it's about conquering yourself."

How do you continue on the path when everything and everybody seems to be an obstacle? Do you remember the Road Runner cartoons? In every episode Wile E. Coyote was out to get the Road Runner. The Wile E. Coyotes of life want to put roadblocks on your path. They complain, try to stop you, and knock you down. In every episode Wile E. Coyote would set a trap only to be caught himself. If you are a coyote trying to keep others down, you'll end up in your own trap. The Road Runners of this world are "Beep Beeping" for the top of the right path. When you are discouraged, think about the Road Runner.

In your travel to the top, don't forget to enjoy the journey. If life is always beep, beep, then it will soon be weep, weep. A dad took his son mountain climbing. It was a tough climb that took all day long. Finally, late in the afternoon they arrived at the top. The father was trying to teach his son the value of hard work and said, "Look at the view. Not many people see this view because they're not willing to put in the hard work to get to the top. We made it and now can enjoy the view." The son replied, "That's great, Dad, it is a beautiful view. But if you had just taken a little time to look while climbing, you would have noticed it was beautiful all the way up." Plan, practice, progress, and persist on your path. Go as far as you can, but don't go so fast that you miss the joy of the journey.

Some Americans, while on a Safari in Africa, learned a valuable lesson. For several days they were guided by African guides, always up early and moving quickly. On the fifth day the Americans were ready to go, but the guides were still asleep. Not understanding, they asked why. The guides said, "We rest and let our souls catch up with our bodies."

Make sure that in your sprint to the top, you don't lose your spirit. The top, even if it has a view of the world, can be empty if only your body arrives. On your path to the top, remember that man does not live by sprint alone.

You've Got Personality

Even as infants, our personalities are evident. Some babies are quiet, calm, and submissive. Others seem to be born with a baseball cap on backwards saying, "Make me."

There are two types of personalities: Type A and Type B. Type A's have a hard time relaxing. One guy's New Year's resolution was "I'm going to learn to relax if I have to spend seven days a week, twenty-four hours a day learning to do it." Now that is not relaxing. Type A's are the hard-driving movers and shakers. They think things like "If I could do this in the microwave, I could do it more quickly." I heard about a guy who put the VCR in the microwave and watched *Gone with the Wind* in fourteen minutes. They switch from lane to lane on the highway and read their mail while talking on the phone. Type A's are very competitive. For instance, when Type A's play in a church softball game, they want to beat the other team to death – in the name of Christian love, of course. If you play ping-pong and suggest playing just for fun – you know – just hit it back and forth – they think you're a communist. Every now and then they stop to smell the roses; then they decide to sell them for Mother's Day. They finish people's sentences, don't listen well, make lists, and like to talk about how much they've done. Their conversation revolves around their accomplishments. "Enough about me, let's talk about you. What do you think about me?"

I love to watch Type A's in the grocery store. They get in the check-out line and of course it's the lane that isn't moving fast enough, so they switch lanes. Naturally, the lane they switch to slows down, and the lane they left speeds up. Then they move between the two lanes – sort of in the middle – waiting until the last minute to see which line goes faster. I have some free advice for Type A's. The law of lines is whichever lane you are in slows down, and whichever lane you switch to slows down. Stay in the first lane; the rest of the world will go faster. I guess you can tell that I have Type A tendencies. I count the number of items in a person's cart if she is in the express lane and go ballistic if someone writes a check in the cash-only line. Type A's spend their lives in the fast lane. The final result is they get to the end more quickly. They concentrate more on what they do instead of who they are and measure themselves by their accomplishments. They are in the express lane to burnout.

The other personality type is Type B. These people don't burn out; they rust out. They write the checks in the express lane. They cause stress for the rest of us. They are so slow they get *USA Yesterday*. If they slowed down any more, they would be in reverse. It takes them two hours to watch *60 Minutes*. They believe the problem with doing nothing is that they can't stop to rest. They have no sense of urgency. They don't have to bring up their accomplishments – they don't have any. Relaxing in a recliner doesn't make them feel guilty. A formal evening includes watching *Wheel of Fortune* with their shoes on. The only word processor they are familiar with is Vanna White. They aren't full of stress, but neither are they full of success.

We are all traveling on the highway of life and trying not to fall into the ditch on either side – the ditch of over-achievement (burnout) or the ditch of apathy (rust out). Some of you are in the fast lane, some are in the slow lane, and some have managed to find the middle. This is neither the fast lane nor the slow lane, but the best lane. This lane – the Type C lane, gives life to words like character, control, compassion, commitment, consistency, continuation, and courage. The key to life is neither to burn out nor to rust out, but to last out. Finish the trip of life on the road that was designed for you. So for all the Type A's, don't forget the rest stops. By the way, since most of you Type A's are leaders – don't forget the people you lead. You may be able to go 100 miles while the people in the back seat just want to find the bathroom. And for all you Type B's, don't forget to make progress. Let's make sure we are in the right lane, and if we see people in the ditch, let's help them out. No matter what your personality, you can take the road best traveled.

3

Hang-ups and Bang-ups of Life

I had a patient who said she had more hang-ups than the phone company. She was right. Her name should have been Ma Bell. These stories are about how to tame your temper, curb your appetite, reject rejection, and a few other things to do before you get out of bed each morning.

'Tis the Season to be Chubby

Most of us gain a little weight over the holidays. Last year my New Year's resolution was to lose some weight. Like most people, the second week of a diet is the easiest because by then I'm off the diet. Many times I go on two diets at the same time so I can get enough food.

But last year I was serious. My body is a temple, but my building program was getting out of control. At first, it was little signs, like the elevator stopping a floor short. Then it was obvious. When I stepped on the scale, the message said, "One at a time, please." Evel Knievel called to see if he could jump over me. Then someone from the government called and said I was being picked up on the satellite photos. I guess the final straw was when I went to McDonald's and got stuck in the golden arches, and the next morning I put my pants on backwards and they fit better. You get the picture. I knew it was time to do something.

I started out with the low-fat cookies for snacks. When you eat low-fat cookies, it's like eating at church. You can eat as many as you want because God doesn't count the calories. So for a snack I would end up eating ten low fat cookies. I later discovered that's 500 calories! I could have had a Snickers! Needless to say, after three weeks I had lost twenty-one...days.

So I got serious and went on a Slim Fast liquid diet. That didn't work well either. It was very difficult – three shakes for breakfast, four shakes for lunch, and two sensible dinners. I still didn't lose any weight.

I tried many diets: the mush diet – you eat while riding on a dog sled; the eggplant diet – plant an egg and whatever comes up, you eat; the vaudeville diet – eat only the foods thrown at you. One time I went on a diet of polyunsaturated oils for two months. I didn't lose any weight, but

I don't squeak anymore. You might achieve the same effect by spraying WD-40 in your ears.

The diet I enjoyed the most was the hole-istic diet. I could eat only doughnut holes. Doughnuts equal fried sugar - *I wonder why they don't put pleasure grams on the side panel of doughnuts.* I gained so much weight on that diet that I decided to cut out breakfast. That morning at work I was so hungry I was chewing my nails. My secretary said, "Your fingernails are a mess!" I said, "You ought to see my feet!"

Then I heard that fiber is the secret. On one diet, you eat the cereal and the box, and after a while you feel like Mr. Ed. This high fiber diet will allow you to live five years longer, but you'll spend four and one-half of those five years in the bathroom.

Since diets weren't going well, I decided I needed to exercise. So I rented the newest exercise video and, unfortunately, I hit the rewind button, worked out in reverse, and gained two pounds.

The older you get, the harder it is to lose weight. Your fat and your body have become friends. It's as if the fat has been living in the same neighborhood for twenty years. It's comfortable there – it doesn't want to leave.

I don't give up easily. My next plan was to find a friend bigger than I am – and I did. It was great! I took him to the ball game because he made a great shade. I don't want to say that he's fat because that is politically incorrect, but he is very "nutritionally enhanced." He measured his diet success by how many chins he'd lost. His telephone number and weight were about the same. He went to Weight Watchers, and the counselors ordered him to leave by the back door.

He's been going to a support group, so I asked him about it. He said every week 200 of the fattest people in the area get in one room and discuss their common problem: How to get out of the room. He does have a good attitude about his weight. He just looks at the positive side of being big: he doesn't need as much water to fill a bathtub; he doesn't fly out of the seat on the roller coaster; and he's easy to spot in a crowd.

People will try just about anything to lose weight. One lady was on a Valium diet. If you take enough Valium, it will help you lose weight. It doesn't really curb your appetite, but most of the food falls on the floor.

My daughter couldn't muster up the will power to lose unwanted pounds. One day, as a friend was coming up the driveway, she said, "Merisa's so skinny it makes me sick." I said, "If it bothers you, why don't you do something about it?" "Good idea," she said, and she hollered at Merisa, "Here, have a Snickers."

The problem is, food has become too important to us. Even when we lose two pounds we celebrate and reward ourselves by going to the pastry shop. I have discovered if it tastes good, spit it out. Food is like anything else in life. If it is really pleasurable from the start, it is probably painful at the end (no pun intended). It's the difference between green beans and jellybeans. If you're going to live ten minutes, have a jellybean, but it's not the food for a lifetime.

Many times we eat the wrong foods because we are eating for the wrong reasons. It may not be what we are eating, but what's eating us. Do you realize that *stressed* spelled backwards is *desserts*? Many times we're hungry, but it's a spiritual hunger which we try to feed with the physical. I've discovered that no amount of Snickers will feed the spirit. I realize that if I eat more soul food, I will be less hungry for Snickers. Bottom line – if eating is the big thing in your life, you will be a big thing.

Rejecting Rejection

I knew a lady who wanted her tombstone to read "To my best friend, my adorable dog, who treated me better than any of my five husbands." Now that was a lady who had experienced rejection. As a psychologist, I work with people who suffer from rejection. One guy said he felt so rejected in childhood that even his invisible friend didn't like him. Inevitably, everyone will be rejected. It's like Ed McMahon stopping at your house to ask for directions. It's meeting the church lady, and instead of hearing her say, "You're special," she says, "You're history." That's rejection.

What are the characteristics of feeling rejected?

Suspicion One guy wouldn't go to football games because he thought the players were talking about him in the huddle. This attitude indicates a lack of trust.

Sensitivity You have to be really careful around sensitive people because they take everything you do personally. It's like the girl whose date is late for dinner. She can think about it in different ways. Positively, she realizes she now has a little more time by herself. Or, neurotically, she can think, "He's trying to get back at me. He's late because he hates me." Some people at the airport are sure the plane is late because the airline hates them. Sensitive people take everything personally.

Self-criticism We get too serious. We look in the mirror so much that we can't take compliments anymore. Someone might say, "Your dress looks nice." Your response: "That old thing! I've had it for years." You put yourself down when people are trying to compliment you. Some pastors are super-spiritual. When a parishioner says, "You preached a great message," the pastor replies, "Well, the Lord did it." You want to say, "The Lord can preach better than that. I was just trying to compliment you." Self-critical people belittle themselves which leads to self-pity. They compare themselves to other people, sometimes irrationally. One guy commented that Shirley McClain remembers things five lifetimes ago. He can't even remember where he put his keys.

Self-isolation Pulling back from people leads to self-destruction. People need people in order to stay healthy, but being rejected doesn't feel good. Frogs are ugly, slow, and low. They droop and look pooped. Frogs look rejected. That's why some of them turn to alcohol. You've seen the commercials. The problem is, alcohol makes life worse because you do dumb things. A drunk phoned in a report that thieves had been in his car. "They stole the dashboard, steering wheel, brake pedal, even the accelerator!" he cried out. However, before the police investigation could start, the phone rang again and the same voice said with a hiccup, "Never mind. I was in the backseat."

Let me tell you how to respond to rejection. Face the fact that people will let you down and that it's usually the result of their own problems. Someone probably stole their lily pad. Don't take it personally.

Have a **do something** mindset. Reject the rejection and decide to do something.

Remember the word **fun**. Loosen up a little bit. Laugh some. Aspirin doesn't cure your illness. It simply raises your threshold of pain and makes you feel as if you are not feeling as bad as you really are. Joy is spiritual aspirin. It raises the threshold of your pain and helps you through difficulties.

Finally, focus on God's unconditional love. People will never be able to give you enough love. If you expect them to, you'll feel rejected and resentful. You'll have bad relationships because people will always disappoint you. Instead, focus on God's unconditional love. A Christmas program featured a six-year-old handicapped boy who had finally gotten up the courage to be in his first recital. As he struggled across the platform, an older boy made a disparaging remark about the boy's handicap. Completely demoralized, that little boy just froze and started to sob. A man rose from his seat and walked to the platform. He knelt beside the boy, put his arm around him, and said to the audience, "It takes a very cruel person to say what was just said to this little boy. He is suffering from something that isn't his fault. This was the first time for him to venture out with his handicap to say anything in public. He's been hurt deeply, but I want you to know that this little boy is my boy. I love him just the way he is. He belongs to me and I'm proud of him." And then he led that little boy off the platform. My friend, that's God. That's unconditional love. Let me give you a personal example. Every leader experiences rejection. I experience it just about every week because I make a decision that people don't like. I couldn't make those hard decisions if I didn't know that when I walk onto the platform, I'm God's little boy. He loves me unconditionally. It doesn't matter what I do or what I say. I'm God's little boy. When you understand that relationship you can handle any kind of rejection.

How do you feel today? Do you feel low, slow, droopy, and pooped? The fairy tale about frogs says a frog is really a prince if only a beautiful lady will kiss him. The only problem is that it is difficult to get a beautiful lady to kiss a frog. But God kisses all of us frogs with His grace and love. When He does, we turn into princes and princesses and realize that we are children of the King. When you understand that, you don't feel low and slow. You begin to feel like God's little boy or girl. That's how to respond to rejection. You may still feel froggy, but remember that Kermit didn't do so bad feeling that way.

Good Forgetters

A man looking through the paper saw an ad he couldn't believe. "For Sale, almost new Jag, loaded, $200." Thinking it was a misprint, he nevertheless called the number. Sure enough the almost brand new Jaguar was loaded and had only 300 miles on it. The woman verified the price and said the first one to her house would get the car. He got there as quickly as he could, saw the car was in mint condition, and thought there must be something wrong with it. He asked, "Ma'am, is it really $200?" She paused and then said, "That might be too much. I'll let you have it for $99.50." He said, "I'll take it, but I'd feel guilty if I didn't tell you it's worth $50,000. Why would you sell it to me for only $99.50?" She said, "My husband ran away with his secretary last week. He just sent me a telegram from Hawaii telling me to sell the Jag and send him the money, and that is exactly what I'm going to do." Forgiveness is often difficult because we want revenge.

A lady, who had never married, carried revenge to her grave. She requested in her will that all the pallbearers at her funeral be female. When the attorney asked why, she said, "Men wouldn't take me out when I was alive, and I'm not going to let them take me out when I'm dead."

Forgiveness is crucial to our happiness, especially within our families because they do the same things over and over again. A young groom realized he had married a door-slammer. She got out of the car and slammed the door; she went into a room and slammed the door. He tried to pretend it didn't bother him, but it was getting to him. Finally, after a very difficult day at work, he heard her slam the outside door, and then she slammed the den door, and then the kitchen door. He jumped up and loudly said, "If you slam another door, I'll scream until the blood runs out of my ears!" She fell apart and cried. He apologized; they talked and worked it out. Then she went to the bathroom and slammed the door.

Why? Because she was a door-slammer; it was her habit. He was going to have to forgive her many times.

It is Hollywood psychobabble to believe that "love is never having to say you're sorry"? Love is not only *saying* we're sorry but also admitting that, at times, we *are* sorry.

A man told me about his wife who, he believed, had never changed a toilet tissue roll since they were married. He got so upset that he started writing the date and time on every cardboard cylinder he changed. One day he had had enough and in his frustration he went to the closet and retrieved two large plastic bags full of cardboard cylinders with the date and time on each one. As he was dumping the cardboard cylinders all over the room he said, "I have proof! I have proof you have never changed the toilet tissue roll." She looked at the cylinders all over the room and said, "You're sick!" He said, "I'll show you who's sick. We're going to see the psychiatrist." He made an appointment to see the psychiatrist, and he and his wife went, carrying the two plastic bags full of cardboard cylinders. The psychiatrist asked, "What seems to be the problem?" The man said, "The problem is that my wife has never changed the toilet tissue roll, and I have proof", and he dumped the cardboard cylinders all over the psychiatrist's desk. The psychiatrist looked at him and said, "You're sick."

We are all sick and defective, and our Maker has recalled every one of us. No one will measure up to your expectations; even you don't measure up to your own expectations. So forgive yourself and forgive others for not being perfect. Be more like children.

I heard about a little boy who was mad at his best friend, Andrew. They got into a fight, and he told his mother, "I hate Andrew, I never want to see him again, and I hope his dog dies." The next day as he was going out to play, his mother asked, "Where are you going?" He said, "I'm going to play with Andrew." She said, "I thought you never wanted to see him again and hoped his dog died." He said, "Yeah, I said that about Andrew, but me and Andrew are good forgetters."

So chill out! Let's be good forgetters, and what you can't forget, forgive. We all carry around our plastic bags full of something, waiting to dump it on the one who has wronged us. Realize that carrying it around does more damage to you than it will do to the person you dump it on. The only way to be laid back is to give up on the payback.

Good and Angry

When a golfer was asked why he bought a new putter, he said, "The old one didn't float." We live in what some people call the age of rage. What about your anger? Do people call you Old Faithful at work, not because you show up everyday but because you blow up every week? Do you want to be known for your anger? When it started to thunder and lightning during a woman's funeral who was known for her temper, her husband said to his son, "Your mother just arrived in Heaven."

You may think you don't have a problem with anger. Are you sure? Sometimes the stoic, silent people are the ones who have the most trouble with anger. They stuff it all inside. Some people handle anger like a turtle: they just pull their head into their shell and pout. Others handle it like skunks: they stink up the environment. Both are inappropriate and both will get you into trouble and keep you from winning in life.

During a race-car event, the second-place car tried to pass the first-place car on the final stretch. The first car drifted inside and forced the challenger into the infield grass. What happened next was incredible. The offended driver pulled his car back onto the track, caught up with the leader and forced him to the outside wall. Both vehicles came to a screeching halt. The two drivers jumped out and quickly got into an old-fashioned slugging match. In the meantime, the third-place driver cruised by for the win. Winners rarely lose their tempers.

Getting angry is like leaping into a fast sports car, gunning the motor, and racing down the highway at high speeds, and then discovering that the car has no brakes. That temperamental personality becomes about 90% temper and 10% mental. You get the Jim Carey syndrome. The madder and madder you get, the dumber and dumber you act.

Anger out of control makes you lose even when you think you've won. At a national park people watched as an enormous bear ate from the trash cans. A skunk ate beside the bear. Someone asked the park ranger, "How does the little skunk get away with eating the garbage around the big black bear?" The ranger replied, "The bear knows the high cost of winning."

Anger, like a loaded gun, is very powerful. If you are careless, you will hurt not only yourself but you will also hurt others. Keep your cool in battle. Don't lose your head, or you'll have no place to put your helmet.

Anger is like an uncontrolled fire in a fireplace. If it gets too big, people are burned. On the other hand, if the fire dies out, the occupants will freeze. The key is adequate respect and adequate control.

Anger can also be your ally if it moves you from apathy to action and energizes you to do things you wouldn't ordinarily do. The emotion of anger can lead to the right motion if you control it and not let it control you. Our nation was born when fifty-six patriots became angry enough to sign the Declaration of Independence.

One lady had many psychiatric problems. One contributing factor was an uncooperative adult son who had been freeloading off her for years. Her physician recommended that she be admitted to a psychiatric hospital. Upon learning this news, her son seemed very pleased at the prospect of getting rid of her and even helped her pack her bags. His attitude made her so furious that she marched back into the house with her luggage and told her son to get out of the house and support himself. The anger forced her to do something that she knew she should have already done. The emotion of anger led to a motion that was good for her.

So it's okay to get good and angry, but be sure you control and channel your anger so others will get the good and not the anger.

Family Feud

Most of us have heard of the feud between the Hatfields and the McCoys. What you might not know is how it all started. In 1878 the two families disputed over the ownership of a hog. That dispute led to a twelve-year war, resulting in the deaths of three Hatfields, seven McCoys, and two outsiders. Disagreement over that one hog took twelve years and twelve lives. Most feuds today are equally ridiculous.

When I was in private practice I was constantly amazed at the reasons people came to see a psychologist. One time, a lady came in for counseling because she was angry over five shirts. *No, I'm serious, that's what she was really ticked off about.* Her husband bought five no-iron shirts. To her, that label meant she didn't have to iron them. But her husband thought she should continue to iron them because he liked the firm crease. The first time they were washed, he didn't wear them, so she asked him why. He said, "Because they aren't ironed." She said, "They don't need to be ironed." They fought over the un-ironed no-iron shirts for months. She came to me and said the problem was five no-iron shirts. I asked, "How long does it take to iron the shirts?" She said, "I guess about three minutes each." I said, "I think I can solve your problem. Next week when you come to see me, bring the five no-iron shirts. I'll bring an ironing board and iron, and I'll iron the shirts for you. It will take about fifteen minutes. While I'm ironing the no-iron shirts, you can sit out in the lobby and have a soft drink and look at magazines. After fifteen minutes I'll have the shirts ready. You'll be happy because you have the shirts ironed. Your husband will be happy because the shirts are ironed. And I'll be happy because I have thirty-five minutes left on a fifty-minute session and I'm making $90. Everyone will be happy." She looked at me and said, "You're an idiot. I'm going to go home and iron the stupid shirts myself." I said, "That's a great idea."

I'm amazed at what people fight over. Two brothers inherited a store from their father. They ran the store together and got along well. One day one of the brothers put a dollar bill on the cash register but didn't have time to come back and get it. When he came back to pick up the dollar, it wasn't there. He said to his brother, "Did you pick up a dollar bill on the register?" The brother said, "No, I didn't pick it up." He said, "You had to pick it up. Nobody else was in the store." The fight escalated until finally they were so angry with each other, they divided the store with a wall, made two separate stores and didn't speak to each other for twenty years. One day a man came into the store and said, "I was in here twenty years ago, I was poor, didn't have a job, and I was hungry. A dollar bill was on the cash register. Nobody was here so I stole it. Now I want to return it. I'll give you whatever interest you'd like." The owner said, "I don't want any interest, but I would like for you to go next door and tell my brother the same story." He went next door, told the brother the story, and then left. As he left he was surprised to see two middle-aged men crying and hugging each other.

Another family feud was over color. In the play, *Philadelphia Here I Come,* a boy from Ireland had a bad relationship with his father, so he decided to go to America to seek his fortune. He went home to say goodbye to his mother and perhaps even talk to his dad, knowing that he would probably never see them again. The talk with his dad didn't go well. The family went to bed. About midnight the father and son were both up for a snack and bumped into each other at the refrigerator. Their inhibitions were down, and they actually began to talk to each other. They began reminiscing about a fishing trip they had taken together when the boy was young. They began to smile and enjoy the conversation. The boy said he would never forget that red boat. Dad interrupted, "No, son, it was a blue boat." They argued about the color of the boat until the relationship had once again been breached. The next morning the son left home. The mother waved goodbye, and the father stayed in the house with his back turned. The father and son never talked again *and the dispute was over the color of a boat*.

We may think, "That's stupid." But the fact is, we fight about things that are just as trivial, almost every day. Let me ask you a question. What one-dollar, no-iron, blue hog are you fighting over? Is it worth it?

Eating Frogs

Procrastination can lead to discouragement and depression. We put off doing something, and then it gets bigger and more difficult so we put it off again. Our philosophy is, "Never put off until tomorrow what you can put off until the day after tomorrow." The molehill becomes a mountain, and you're really depressed. My advice is – just do it. If you have to eat a bunch of frogs, go ahead and eat the big one first. Get it over with.

When I practiced psychology, people often told me that they were too depressed to get out of bed. I would say, "You have to get out of bed." They would say, "I'm too depressed. How do I get out of bed?" I would say, "Take one foot and put it on the floor and stand up. That's how you get out of bed. Do it." I've done it. I've gone to work depressed. I've given speeches depressed. I can't tell someone to announce, "Charles is depressed, so we won't have a speaker today." I think I've even spoken on depression while depressed.

A colleague of mine had a patient who was a college student who was depressed because she couldn't seem to get her homework done. She came to see him and instead of doing psychotherapy with her and having her lie on the sofa and talk about her mother, he suggested they work on homework for the first thirty minutes and then talk the next thirty minutes. He found that when she finished her homework, she wasn't as depressed. When she got something done, she felt better about herself.

A farmer in Tennessee commented that lightning had struck an old shed and relieved him of having to tear it down. The rain washed off his car and saved him from that chore too. When asked what he was doing now, he replied, "Waiting for an earthquake to shake the potatoes out of the ground."

What are you waiting for? The time to fix the roof is when the sun is shining. There is a difference between living in the waiting room and waiting in the living room. "One of these days" is "none of these days." Whatever sits on the shelf rots. There are no perfect and ideal situations. You may end up like the young man who vowed never to marry until he found the ideal woman. Unfortunately when he found her she was waiting for the ideal man. One cannot wait until the entire army is in perfect condition before facing the enemy. General McClellan was waiting for the army to get ready during the first year of the Civil War. President Lincoln asked if he might borrow the army if McClellan weren't going to use it.

Abraham didn't have a destination, but he packed up and left home. Moses didn't have a clue, yet he walked into Pharaoh's palace. If you wait until you're sure, you'll never take off your training wheels.

Three turtles went on a Sunday afternoon picnic. One carried the basket of food, one carried a jug of turtleade, and the third turtle didn't carry anything. They set up the picnic and then felt raindrops. The two turtles agreed that the one who carried nothing should go back and get the umbrella. The third turtle said, "No, because you'll eat all the turtle food and drink all the turtleade and there won't be any left for me." Finally, he agreed to go back for the umbrella. One hour, two hours, three hours went by and finally one day, one week, and two weeks. One of the turtles said, "Well, I guess we can eat the turtle food and drink the turtleade because he's not coming back." Then they heard something over in the bushes say, "If you do, I won't go."

Most of us are like the turtle. We're afraid that if we jump out there and do something, we might miss the picnic. The truth is, we will miss the picnic by not trusting God and not doing our part. Don't you think it's time to take off the training wheels?

De-scenting a Skunk

Everyone has conflicts. After the first fight my wife and I had, I didn't see her for a couple of days, and then slowly my left eye began to open. Now my eyes are wide open and I realize that conflict is inevitable.

One couple had been arguing about anything and everything for years. They were tired of living in a perpetual state of conflict. Finally she told her husband about the prayer she was praying. She said, "I've been asking God to help us stop all this arguing by taking one of us to heaven. When he answers my prayer, I'm moving in with my sister." Well, I doubt God is going to answer that kind of prayer. God wants us to avoid conflict when the situation isn't worth it. A bulldog can whip a skunk, but it's not worth it. Most of the time, however, avoiding conflict is like avoiding termites. Eventually it will bring the house down.

One way to solve conflict is to avoid a middleman. I heard a story out of Texas, so it may or may not be true, about a bank robber named Jorge Rodriguez, who operated along the Texas border around the turn of the century. He was so successful in his forays that the Texas Rangers put an extra posse along the Rio Grande to stop him. Sure enough, late one afternoon, one of these special Rangers saw Jorge Rodriguez stealthily slipping across the river. The Ranger trailed him at a discreet distance as he returned to his home village. He watched Jorge mingle with the people in the square and then go into his favorite cantina to relax. The Ranger slipped in to get the drop on Jorge. With a pistol in his hand he said, "I know who you are, Jorge Rodriguez, and I have come to get back all the money you have stolen from the banks in Texas. Unless you give it to me, I'm going to blow your brains out." There was one fatal difficulty, however; Jorge didn't speak English, and the Texas Ranger was not versed in Spanish. They were two adults in a verbal impasse. But about that time an enterprising man said, "I am bilingual. Do you want me to act as translator?" The Ranger nodded and the little man put the words of the Ranger into terms that Jorge could understand. Nervously, Jorge answered back, "Tell the big Texas Ranger that I have not spent a cent of the money. If he will go to the well in the Town Square, face north, count down five stones, he will find a loose stone. Pull it out and all the money is behind it. Please tell him quickly." The translator got a solemn look on his face and said to the Ranger in perfect English, "Jorge Rodriguez is a brave man. He says he is ready to die." Solve conflict by talking about it to the one you have the conflict with.

Think of three words when solving conflict: information, reconciliation, and understanding. The first word is information. Many times just a little more information will help solve a problem. Such was the case with a group of soldiers from Nepal who fought on the side of Britain against Indonesia. This regiment was not trained to be paratroopers, but a particular mission required that they parachute into a remote location. The British asked them to volunteer to jump for this mission, but they refused. Later they sent word to the British that they would accept the mission under certain conditions. The first condition was that the area in which they were to land be reasonably soft, and the second was that the plane would have to fly as slow as possible and at an altitude of only 100 feet. The British said the planes always fly as slow as possible during jumps, but they wouldn't be able to fly 100 feet from the ground because at such a low altitude there is not sufficient time for the parachutes to open. "Parachutes?" they exclaimed, "We get parachutes?" These brave soldiers did not know they would have parachutes. They were willing to jump from the plane wherever and however the mission required. A little information can make the difference. It can change hesitation into participation, fear into courage, and "no" to "yes." Take the time to communicate. People might even jump out of an airplane for you.

Information is important and so is reconciliation, the second word. But often, resolution is impossible because no matter how much you talk, you will never see eye to eye. So decide that you will still walk hand in hand, unless the person really is a skunk. Then you might try to convince him to jump out of the airplane. Just kidding. Even the skunks of the world deserve love.

Conflict resolution also requires understanding, the third word. A boy stood at the side of the highway throwing clumps of mud at the cars passing by. Finally, one irate driver stopped, got out of the car, and yelled, "Hey kid, what's the idea?" Before he could say anything else the boy said, "Thank you for stopping. I've tried to wave others down, but no one would stop. My dad and I were camping, and he's hurt badly. He's over here in the brush. Please help us." Sometimes when people throw mud at you, they are really crying for help.

So next time you have a conflict with someone, think of information, reconciliation, and understanding. That skunk may just be crying out for help. Even if he or she is a skunk, think cocker spaniel instead of bulldog.

Dead Ends and Runways

John Madden, of CBS Sports, crisscrosses the country many times each fall by bus because he's afraid of flying. There's a lot of fear in this world. I sat beside a lady on a plane who had never flown before, and she was scared to death. She was very excited when she found out that I was a psychologist who worked for a church. I told her everything would be okay because "up there" we'd be close to the home office. What I noticed was that her fear was contagious. The more she talked, the more afraid I started to get. I forgot to put my tray table in its upright and locked position, and the flight attendant gave me that look, so I immediately put it up. Then I started wondering why putting the tray table up was such a big deal? I have never read about a plane crash where the ones killed were the only ones who forgot to put their tray tables in the upright and locked position.

Then I started listening to the flight attendant talk about the exit doors: "The white lights lead to the red lights that lead to the exit doors." At 38,000 feet I'm thinking, "Why do I need the exit doors?" Then I'm told that I have a flotation device under my seat. We're flying over New Mexico; it's all desert! People say that in Albuquerque, when we had the big flood (you know, as in Noah) we got only four inches. It's so dry the cows have to graze 60 mph to keep from starving to death, and they produce powdered milk. I don't need a flotation device under my seat. I need a parachute!

Then I started thinking about "airplane poison" – one drop will kill you. I thought about all the crashes I've read about. They always talk about those black boxes made out of indestructible material. I wonder why they don't make airplanes out of that material. I remember the old preacher who wouldn't fly because he said the Lord said, "*Lo*, I am with you always," not high.

Now *I'm* frightened. I'm focused on my fears instead of my faith. We are ready to take off. I look down that long runway. I see that it's really just a short road that leads nowhere. If I were in a car, I would call this runway a dead end. But I'm in a plane, not a car, and this plane has enough power to overcome that dead end and make it a runway to many wonderful things God has in store for me.

I guess that may be the difference between faith and fear. Fear is seeing situations as dead end. This will be the end of me. Faith is seeing dead-ends as runways. This could be the beginning of something great. You must have the faith to believe there will be enough power when you come to a dead end.

It's always been that way. Twelve spies went out to see the Promised Land. Ten saw giants and two saw God. Ten saw a dead end, and two saw a runway to the biggest grapes they'd ever seen. By the way, grapes and giants often come together. You're not going to get the good stuff (grapes) without facing your fears (giants). Faith is seeing God in every situation and believing He has the power to turn every dead end into a runway.

Well, it was take-off time. The lady beside me was talking nervously about all her fears. Now I was ready, not only to take off, but also to share my faith with my new friend. When people share their fears with you, share your faith with them. It's God's way of keeping your concentration on the runway instead of the dead end. Put your tray table in its upright and locked position and prepare to eat airplane food. Now that's something to be afraid of.

The "BEAR" Facts of Fear

I went to college at a small, conservative school. My dad wanted me there because it was supposedly 100 miles from any known sin. Part of the process for freshmen was Rat Week. Each freshman was assigned to a Rat Daddy, a sophomore, and the freshman had to do everything he said the first semester. It was a horrible experience. My particular Rat Daddy told me there was only one way to get out of this torture. I had to steal the Rat Hat off the biggest freshman and give it to him. I thought that was a good idea and I was determined to get it done. The biggest freshman was Big John, six foot six inches, and 260 pounds. I managed to get his hat, and as I ran I could hear him screaming. But Big John didn't know who had stolen his hat. My roommate said, "I hope he never finds out." I said, "Well, how will he ever find out? Only you and I know." Then I started to worry. My roommate never told him, but the whole year it seemed as if Big John was everywhere I went. I kept looking over my shoulder for him and wondering if he knew, and, if he did, what he might do to me. He made my life miserable, and he didn't even know it. Fear affects your behavior and your relationships. About ten years ago, someone who had also gone to my school told me that Big John had died. I felt relieved. Now that's unhealthy.

Unhealthy reactions to fear usually lead to escapism and exaggeration. Escapism is when you are trying to get out of a situation. It's like the old mountaineer who came home one day with his clothes torn and shoes worn, looking totally exhausted. He had been gone for over a week. His wife said, "Where in tarnation have you been?" He said, "Well, I went out to check on the cows, and all of a sudden this giant bear jumped out, the biggest bear I've ever seen in my life, and I ran like crazy until I finally lost the bear. I've never run faster in my whole life." His wife replied, "You've been gone for a week. Where have you been since then?" He said, "I was walking back." That's escapism.

Exaggeration is when you blow fear out of proportion. It's like the guy who says the only way he got away from a bear was by his quick thinking. He was out picking blackberries when the bear began to chase him. He ran, but periodically he dropped a few berries for the bear to eat and then he would get ahead. Eventually the bear would catch up, and he would repeat the process. Then he saw a frozen lake, and he ran out on the frozen ice. When the bear chased him, the bear's weight caused him to fall in and drown. The man's friend who was listening to the story said, "That's impossible. You cannot pick blackberries and be on a frozen lake at the same time of the year." The man said, "It did happen. The bear chased me from July to January." That's exaggeration.

Now that you have the "bear" facts about escapism and exaggeration, let me tell you that you also don't need a rabbit's foot because it didn't do the rabbit much good either. What you need to do is face your fears. When you face your fears, you generate energy. Facing fear turns fear into fuel for your faith so you can act in a constructive way.

The story is told about a football game in which Coach Bear Bryant was trying to hold on to a one-point lead. With two minutes to play he called on his small but slow, fourth-string quarterback. Bryant instructed him to run the ball up the middle and then punt. The new quarterback stunned the opposition with several first-down runs. Deep in his opponent's territory, temptation overcame instruction. He had never had an opportunity to throw a touchdown pass, so, disregarding his coach, he threw the ball. The opposing safety intercepted the pass and broke into the clear. The sluggish quarterback struggled to his feet, started chasing the safety, who happened to be the fastest man on the field, and tackled him before he crossed the goal line. The gun sounded, ending the game. When the two coaches met at mid-field, Bryant's competitor shook his head in disbelief. "How could a fourth-string quarterback catch my fastest safety?" he quizzed. "That's easy," Bryant responded. "Your man was running for a touchdown. My man was running for his life."

F.E.A.R. – Face, Energize, Act, and Realize. Fear energizes and pumps adrenaline, allowing us to do what we could not otherwise do. Facing our fears causes us to act. Then we realize our fear is fuel for faith, and we run for the life that God created for us.

Confusing World

It's a confusing world. Have you looked around lately? Boys want to be girls, girls want to be boys, and Michael Jackson wants to be both. Can you remember when picking a member of the opposite sex was not multiple choice? Can you remember when women wore gloves and dentists didn't? Can you believe that you can get the same graduation present for both males and females – earrings? I went to a wedding, and the pastor said to the groom, "Now you may take the ring out of your nose and put it on her finger." Teenagers are confused, but adults are just as confused. They don't know what they want to do with their lives. That's why they're always asking kids, "What do you want to do when you grow up?" They're looking for ideas!

Where do you look for help? Some people look to churches. Some churches are confused themselves. I saw a church the other day that, instead of having a steeple on top, had a question mark. Maybe people go there to make a "confusion of faith." People look to the psychiatric clinics. I have a Ph.D. in psychology, and, having worked in the clinic, I know it's a study of the id by the odd. I left the psychiatric clinic – I couldn't tell the patients from the staff, except that the staff had keys. Well, actually, they wanted me to leave. I think I became too direct. I told the truth, like, "It is as bad as you think it is," or "They really are out to get you." One patient said he was a loser because his dad was an alcoholic. I said, "Why don't we look at this another way? Maybe your dad's an alcoholic because you're a loser." People won't pay money for that kind of advice. I went from a psychiatric clinic to directing a counseling center at a church. People asked if that was a big adjustment. I said no, not really. The staff still has the keys.

People are so confused today that they even call the psychic hotline. You've probably seen the ad: If you need help call this number. If they were really psychic, they'd call you. I heard Psychic Friends Network went bankrupt. You'd think they would have seen it coming.

Some people look for help from the New Age Movement. Shirley MacLaine says she can help. At a recent Hollywood banquet Shirley won seven lifetime achievement awards. She's the spokesperson for the New Age Movement. People pay for her seminar in which she says she cleanses the seven energy centers of the body. It's like buying a $400 bottle of metaphysical Milk of Magnesia. She ought to be spokesperson for London Fog.

All I hear about these days is the information highway and computers. The terms are confusing. My wife said she wanted software for Christmas, and I got her lingerie. My staff said I had a megabyte, so I went to the orthodontist. They say the information highway's going to change the whole world. Predictions are that there'll be a computer in every home. That way the homes can be just as confused as the offices.

Even if I could speed down the informational highway, where does it lead? Americans don't believe in going anywhere slowly, so we're going nowhere fast.

People are confused, not from lack of information, but from lack of inspiration. They know what to do; they just don't have the power to do it. They would like to stay married to the same person; they just don't have the power to do it. They would like to stay off drugs; they just don't have the power to do it. We could go on and on.

Confusion, that's what I see. Confusion is like a sheep without a shepherd. Now, where have I heard that before?

Battling the Blues

Life has its great times, its average times, and its rough times. Mountains always have valleys. The old preacher said, "Sometimes I'm up, sometimes I'm down, and sometimes I'm almost to the ground." Usually we feel as if we're on the fast track and other times on the slow track, but sometimes we feel as if we're tied to the track. Those are the times when we're helpless, hopeless, hurt, and humorless. We have all been there. People have different names for it. The Apostle Paul called it losing heart, one pastor called it low tide, another called it the minister's fainting fits, the Psalmist called it the depths, the poet called it the dark night of the soul, psychologists call it depression, and I call it Monday. It's the down time.

Everyone has bad days. One guy's love life was so bad he tried to place an ad in the personals, and the newspaper accidentally put it in the obituaries. Even Robert Schuller of the Crystal Cathedral, the positive preacher of the possibility persuasion, probably has bad days. I'm sure he checks into a hotel under an assumed name and says all day long, "I hate glass and Windex." In the same motel are Zig Ziglar thinking negative thoughts, Rush Limbaugh thinking liberal thoughts, and Rick Warren with no purpose whatsoever. Britney Spears checks in and puts on clothes. Everybody has bad days.

When you got up this morning did you sing "Oh What A Beautiful Morning," or did you sing "Make the World Go Away?" Did your Ivory soap sink? Then you may have the blues.

How do you battle the blues? First, you grow up and prepare for difficult times. Unless you're Superman, you will have some wrecks.

When Muhammad Ali was in his prime, about to take off on an airplane, a flight attendant reminded him to fasten his seatbelt. He replied brashly, "Superman don't need no seatbelt." The flight attendant quickly answered, "Superman don't need no airplane, either." Ali fastened his seatbelt.

Let's see if any of you are Superman. Can you leap tall buildings in a single bound? Are you faster than a speeding bullet? Are you more powerful than a locomotive? Are you Superman? No? Then don't go through life thinking you are. Prepare for the wrecks of life. Your seatbelt will wrinkle your shirt, but so will the windshield.

Grow up and don't give up. A very eccentric inventor created a beverage. Everyone who tried it told him how great it was and that he ought to market and sell it. He got excited, formed a company, came up with a marketing plan, and called his drink 4-UP, but nobody bought it. He got a little discouraged, but he hired a different marketing director, added more sugar, less fizz, and called it 5-UP. Once again, nobody bought it. He was still discouraged, but he went back and tried it again and this time he called it 6-UP, but still no takers. Completely discouraged he quit. If only he knew how close he was to 7-UP. Don't give up. Think up. Think 7-UP.

Grow up, don't give up, and keep moving. When you have the blues you tend to isolate yourself, stay home, eat, watch Jerry Springer, and tell yourself you'll get better. You won't. You can't feel your way out of the blues; you act your way out of the blues.

A pastor was visiting the terminally ill ward at the hospital and asked three guys what they wanted said at their funeral. The first said, "Tell them the guy in the casket was a good family man." The second guy said to say, "The guy in the casket was a loyal husband." The third guy said, "At my funeral I want you to look down at my casket and say 'That guy...that guy is moving!'"

Keep moving. Go to work depressed, but go. Most of life is just showing up. Grow up, don't give up, show up, and look up.

A young husband's wife died and left him with a small son. After the funeral the boy asked if he could sleep with his dad. When the man turned off the lights the boy said, "It's so dark I can't see you. Daddy, is your face toward me?" His father realized he had his back to his son so he rolled over and put his face very close to his son's and whispered, "Yes, my face is toward you."

It doesn't matter how dark it gets; by faith look up. God's face is toward you.

To Err is Human – Mistake or Masterpeace?

We all make mistakes. That's why we have are erasers on pencils, reverse gears in cars, delete keys on computers, U-turns, and summer school.

One of my favorite presidents was Gerald Ford. One reason that I liked him was that he was a lousy golfer. The newscasts often showed clips of people being hit by his golf ball. He was so bad at golf that when he hit a shot people yelled "eight" instead of "fore." He made other mistakes as well. One day he arrived at Orly airport in France in front of 800 elite French troops in their uniforms, the entire diplomatic Corp, and President Pompidou. Ford stepped out of the plane, waved to the crowd, and tumbled down the stairs. A tissue was offered and declined. He got up, laughed, brushed off his clothes, strolled forward with a big smile, and took the arm of the Spanish ambassador who was standing next to Pompidou. He walked off with him down the red carpet leaving Pompidou staring after him in amazement. We all make mistakes, even Presidents.

The more new things you try, the more mistakes you're likely to make. One father says that every time his son drives the car it's like starting a new paragraph. He always indents.

Then, of course, plenty of people love to point out our mistakes. A businesswoman stopped at a coffee shop and ordered a cup of coffee. The waitress grudgingly delivered it and asked, "Anything else?" "Yes," said the businesswoman, "I'd like some sugar, cream, a spoon, a napkin, and a saucer for the cup." "Well, aren't you the demanding one," the waitress said. "Look at it from my point of view," the businesswoman said, "You served a cup of coffee and made five mistakes."

We overlook mistakes when it is to our advantage. I heard about a guy who was overpaid at work by a huge sum of money, but he didn't say anything. A couple of weeks later, he was underpaid. He went in and said, "Look, I was underpaid this week." They said, "Yes, but last week we overpaid you, and you didn't say anything." He said, "Well, I figure everybody's entitled to one mistake. Since you made two, I thought I should let you know."

Some mistakes are stupid, like the man who was arrested in Wichita, Kansas, for trying to pass counterfeit money at an airport hotel. The counterfeit loot was two $16 bills. Some mistakes hurt, like the guy who didn't pay enough postage on a letter bomb. It came back with "return to sender" stamped on it. Forgetting it was a bomb, he opened it.

Yes, your mistakes can hurt, and other people's mistakes can also hurt. A pair of Michigan robbers entered a record shop nervously waving revolvers. The first one shouted, "Nobody move!" When his partner moved the startled bandit shot him.

The first thing to do when you make a mistake is to admit it. As a female shopper exited a convenience store, a man grabbed her purse and ran. The clerk called 911 immediately, and the woman was able to give the police a detailed description of the snatcher. Within minutes, the police had apprehended the thief. They put him in the car and drove back to the store. The man was taken out of the car and told to stand for a positive ID. To which he replied "Yes, Officer. That's her. That's the lady I stole the purse from."

We can learn from our mistakes, but we can also profit from our mistakes. Although his daughter's name is today more widely recognized than his, a famed ventriloquist would have died in obscurity had he not learned to profit from his mistakes. This young boy was very interested in photography, so he dutifully saved his money to buy a photography book from a mail-order catalog. The publisher made a mistake with the order and sent a book on ventriloquism instead. The boy had no idea what the book was about and was saddened that he had not received his long-anticipated book on photography. He didn't know he could return the book, so he kept it and began to read about a subject of which he had never heard. His interest grew, and he soon learned to masterfully throw his voice. He eventually got a dummy that he named Charlie McCarthy, and Edgar Bergen was on his way to international fame. Needless to say, his daughter, Candice Bergen, has enjoyed the fame of that name as well. And it all started with a mistake.

I would be mistaken if I didn't point out that mistakes could become masterpieces. A tourist in the Orient noticed an unusual training session and stopped to observe. A master weaver was working on a large piece of tapestry, and behind him stood ten apprentice weavers in a semicircle working on their own similar projects. As the master wove a pattern, the apprentices very carefully copied him, trying to duplicate the same pattern. When an apprentice would make a mistake, the master weaver would walk over to his place, very intently study his pattern and then began to weave an entirely different pattern. Using the mistake the apprentice had made, he turned it into a masterpiece.

So, as you go through a life of mistakes, don't suffer from mistaken identity. Identify those mistakes you don't want to repeat, those you can learn from, and those that, with some help from the Master, could be the peace your life's puzzle needs.

4

Family Time

Family is a great word. If it were a movie, it would be called "Close Encounters of the Right Kind." Life at close quarters can yield million dollar results. Of course, raising three daughters can also leave you bankrupt. So this happy, but broke, author encourages you to read about the family.

Calling All Dads

Being a father is like playing golf. It's time consuming, expensive, frustrating, and full of hazards. The Illinois Telephone Company reports that calls made on Father's Day are growing faster than those on Mother's Day. The company apologized for the delay in compiling this statistic. Everything slowed down because of the extra billing; most of the calls were collect. That seems to be the way it works. First, your kids call you Dada, then Daddy, then Dad, and then they call you collect. Father actually comes from the Greek word *fedoras* – one with deep pockets. Even Santa Claus gets in the house through Dad's wallet.

One way to be a good father is to just follow directions. A father of five came home with a new toy. He summoned his children and asked which one of them should be given the present. "Who is the most obedient and never talks back to mother and does everything he or she is told?" he inquired. There was silence, then a chorus of voices said, "You play with it, Daddy."

Fathering is more confusing than it used to be. Things have even changed on the playground. Kids talk differently. They used to say, "My dad can beat-up your dad." Now they either say, "My dad is your dad, stupid," or "Big deal, so can my mom." Being a father is also scary. I remember getting a card from my youngest daughter, Breanne, right after she got her driver's license. It said, "Dad, you taught me a lot of things over the years. But one thing I learned all by myself…Your car won't go over 100 mph." That's scary.

Teenagers make fatherhood particularly tough. One father told his daughter she could date after her sixteenth birthday, which was in February. It was December and she wanted to go to the Christmas prom. She said some hunk had asked her out on a date and she pleaded with her dad, "Daddy, couldn't we just move it up a little bit? I'm almost sixteen." They had a long talk and finally he said, "No, you can't. You're not sixteen yet and you can't go." Well, you know how kids are at that age. She looked him right in the eye and said, "Daddy, do you believe in the Second Coming of Jesus Christ?" He said, "Of course I do." She said, "I'll tell you what I'm praying for. I pray that Jesus comes back before my sixteenth birthday so you'll have to spend the whole of eternity knowing that your daughter never had a date."

Most fathers feel like a fool instead of cool. A college professor came home after a date with his wife. While the babysitter had been preoccupied, his son located the electric shaver and put a runway down the middle of his head. His father was livid. This well educated man was also bald, by the way, not a hair on his head. He said, "Didn't I tell you to never touch my shaver? You're going to get the spanking of your life." Just as he started to swat him, his son said, "Wait until you see Sister." The man stopped and called his daughter. She appeared without a hair on her head – totally bald. He couldn't believe it. He exclaimed, "How could you do this?" In unison they said, "Dad, we just wanted to look like you."

It's even more confusing when we give our children good advice and set a bad example. One little kid wrecked his tricycle and came running in to his dad and said, "Dad, I've wrecked my tricycle. What's the word you say when you hit the golf ball bad?"

Let me tell you about the time that I quit smoking cigars. Angela was about five years old. I was finishing my Ph.D. in psychology and feeling like Freud. I used to like to eat a big meal and smoke a cigar. We had gone to the beach to take a break. Sitting out on the porch after the big evening meal, I had a big cigar. I'd smoke the cigar and then set it down and pick it up, etc. My wife nudged me because, one time when I put it down, Angela picked it up. She was smoking the cigar. It wasn't funny seeing a five-year-old kid smoking a cigar. Why did I quit? Because it didn't matter what I said; it mattered what I did.

So, Dads, instead of cramming things down your kids' throats, just lay it on their hearts. They'll watch you and in about twenty-five years or so, they'll look back and that fool will be cool. And on Father's Day they might even call to tell you so – collect, of course.

Teenagers

What happened? You put them to bed normal, and they wake up weird. They become teenagers. They dress for school, and they look like a Groucho Marx comedy team. You meet their friends and you want to say, "Pick a gender and stick with it and buy some pants that fit." What do you do? Sell them to the zoo?

God gives us twelve years to love our children before He turns them into teenagers. If kids were born teenagers, we might kill them. God knew that, so He gave us twelve years to build a bond of love so when they are teenagers, even though we'd like to kill them, we don't. God is smart.

Teenagers are hard to understand. When our daughter turned thirteen, my wife said, "I need a Bible verse to get me through the teen years." If you look up "teenager" in the Bible, it isn't there. I finally referred her to Luke 2:50, "And they [Jesus' parents] understood not the saying which he spoke to them." Penny was disappointed; she didn't like my suggestion. I had to explain that Jesus' parents couldn't understand Him either. Everything was fine until He hit the teen years and didn't go home from the synagogue with them. He decided to stay a few more days, with or without His parents. Don't you know they were ticked, or in the King James Version, "wrought"? You think you have stress with your teenager; think about poor Mary – she thought she had lost the Son of God.

I know I would have been wrought (ticked off). The problem is teenagers are half child and half adult. They say, "Don't tell me what to do," and thirty minutes later they ask, "What should I do?" Of course, I heard of one teenager who said, "No one is going to tell me what to do; I'm going to join the Marines."

I try to think back to when I was a teenager. Was I this uncooperative? Was my IQ ever equal to that of plant life? Did I ever have that urge to merge? Yes, maybe I did. I can remember those trips with Mom downtown to exotic places like Cloth World, and I did act pretty badly.

I've discovered it may be easier to be the teenager than the parent. Legend has it that one day St. Peter passed a blind man, and he healed him. He passed a lame man, and he healed him. He came to a man who was crying, and St. Peter asked him what his problem was. He said, "I'm the father of a teenager." St. Peter sat down and wept with him.

We'll try anything to control our teenagers. We even put words in God's mouth. One father told his son if he would go to all of his classes, get all A's and B's, and cut his hair, he would buy him a car. At the end of the year, the teenager came in, showed his dad his report card and said, "I went to all my classes and got all A's and B's, and I want my car." The dad said, "But son, you haven't cut your hair." The boy said, "Dad, even Jesus had long hair." And the father said, "Yes, and that's why Mary and Joseph never bought him a car. He had to walk everywhere He went."

I know teenagers can be exasperating. For one birthday I received cuff links, and my teenager said, "I know they aren't much, but that's all you could afford."

What do you do when you are the discouraged parent of teenagers? Remember first that they are God's children, not yours. Also, remember that even God (the perfect parent) had problems with the first two kids

(Adam and Eve). Get off your guilt trip. Remember that everything comes to pass; nothing comes to stay. The teenage years will pass.

Now if these things don't encourage you, then think of this and smile: one day your children will have teenagers of their own.

You're Wonderful!

Like most families, we went on vacation and drove 500 miles to look for a place that served home-cooked meals. We stopped to get our fix of southern cooking. Our waiter was service-industry challenged. He couldn't get anything right. I thought, "If he gets minimum wage, he's overpaid." The experts say that an average person only uses 10% of his brain. In this case the kid was way below average. His IQ was so low I thought he would stumble on it just walking out to help us. He needed some industrial strength counseling on customer service.

The worse the service was, the more irritated I became. When I'm irritated, I use humor to make sure people understand I'm irritated. When the waiter came by, I said, "You've been gone so long, I expected a much older guy to come back." My wife and daughters were getting irritated with me because they knew I was irritated with him. So they kicked me under the table and said, "Act like a Christian." I told them that I was on vacation, but it didn't seem to make any difference to them.

As the meal progressed, I noticed something different in the way my family interacted with the waiter and the way I interacted with him. They didn't look at his performance; they looked at him as a person. They thought this guy was wonderful. They asked him questions and found out he was married, and that he and his wife were expecting a baby. They found out that this was his first job. I could've told them that much. They looked at his person instead of his performance.

When we got ready to leave, my family told me to leave him a big tip. They have always been very generous with my money. So I gave a $10 tip on a $25 meal, and they wrote on the ticket, "God loves you and so do we." Now, would I have done that on my own? No. But I discovered something by watching what took place. When they focused on him as a person, his performance improved. And I've noticed in life that when you focus on a person's strengths, his weaknesses start to improve.

That day with my family reminds me of a story about a man who was promoted to manager of a logging camp. He asked the former boss if he had the power to hire and fire. The former boss said, "You want to fire Tony, don't you?" The man said, "Yes, I do." Then the former boss said, "Now that you are in charge, you may fire Tony if you want, but I should tell you that he's one of your best workers. His group has the best record of any other group. You can fire Tony, but you'll fire one of the best."

The next day the new manager called a meeting, told everyone he had been promoted and he could hire and fire. After the meeting was over, Tony went to the new boss and said, "You're going to fire me, aren't you?" His boss said, "Well, I was going to, but your old boss said you're wonderful. He said you are the best worker that I have, so I'm not going to fire you." Tony wasn't prepared for this response and the boss wasn't prepared for Tony's reaction. Tony had a tear in his eye, and as he walked away he mumbled, "Why didn't he ever tell me that? Why didn't he ever tell me?" Tony's life was changed that day. He eventually became president of one of the largest logging companies in America and it all started the day he found out what the boss thought about him.

I suspect Tony's boss learned the same lesson I learned from my girls. Wonderful performance comes from people who believe someone thinks they are wonderful. If you're discouraged with your performance, remember the boss, God, thinks you're wonderful.

Through the Nose, from the Heart

Conceiving a child is gloriously cost-free, but the meter starts to run immediately and never seems to stop. Even the gifts given to me, I buy. Christmas comes every year, and the only way Santa Claus can get into the house is through Dad's wallet. My family always tells me they don't overspend I just under-deposit. One year for Father's Day my card read, "I couldn't decide what card to give you; your VISA, American Express, or Master Card."

I guess my advice is that if you are going to have children, examine your nose because you're going to be paying through it for the rest of your life. Actually, financially it isn't that costly. We were broke when we had our kids, and now they're grown and we're still broke, so it must not cost that much.

If any children are reading this book, be kind to your parents. After they raise you and send you through college, you're all they have left. Remember that fifth commandment: Humor your parents.

There are some other costs involved in raising children. One is that your clothes will never be the same. Children have a large drool gland that will produce that not-so-stylish wet-shoulder look. And there are emergencies, like on a trip, when a kid says, "I feel sick." Stop the car and run. Speaking of trips, they will be less stressful and cost you less energy if you never have more children than your car has windows. Then there are the countless diaper changes. My advice here is never change diapers in midstream.

Children cost you your bathroom. With three daughters, I hid all our valuables in the bathroom because I knew no thief could ever get in there. The definition of a dirty old man is a middle-aged father with three daughters and one bathroom. I've heard rumors that teenage boys are just as bad. When daughters leave home, you don't lose a daughter; you gain a bathroom and a phone.

Raising kids also costs you a clean house. Children are messy. They destroy a house before you can say, "Get in your room." Their plan is to mess up the whole house so that Mom will never notice their rooms.

They cost you your privacy. Remember that out of the mouths of children will come words that Dad should have never said. Like the time, when after stumbling over the same toy that was left out for the millionth time, I explained the origin of fallen angels. One day when God was walking around in heaven He stumbled on a toy the angels had left out. When God told them to pick up their toys, some of the angels didn't, so God started hell. It seemed like a great way to get the kids to pick up their toys until my daughter shared this basic theology with her Sunday School class. The pastor gave me a call.

Kids cost you your pride. Many times I felt like a nanny trying to help raise my girls. Then the teenage years hit. It happened so fast. During the teenage years I felt more like a ninny than a nanny. Like the time when my oldest daughter, Angela, had to have that special dress for her big night. I can remember it well. As a matter of fact, the whole family can remember my reaction well. It was the first time she actually picked out and purchased an expensive dress – I use the word purchased loosely – she charged it to *my* account. (Money isn't everything, but it does keep you in touch with your children, especially as they get older.)

I didn't handle the dress incident too well. The price was high and the material seemed nonexistent. It appeared she paid $10 an inch for the material because the whole dress had only about fifteen inches of material. She modeled the dress for me and I went ballistic. I told her she had bought an upside-down-dress. Instead of having a high top and low bottom it had a low top and high bottom. I told her she wasn't in the dress far enough. For once I became over generous. Money was no object. Buy more material!

Raising children can cost you your identity. There was a time when my daughter, Kasey, went through the stage of calling my wife and me by our first names instead of Mom and Dad. Penny went along with it, but I couldn't handle it. I told her if she called me Charles I would call her "Carless." She asked what I meant. I said, "For one thing you haven't known me long enough to call me Charles, and for another, Charles doesn't give cars; only Dad does. If I'm just Charles to you, you don't have a car anymore. They could even make a movie about you, 'Rebel Without a Car.'" The next day, Charles became Dad again.

There is the final cost – the wedding. Someone asked me what part I performed in the wedding. I just had a small part – I was the Maid of Debt. All I had to do was answer the question, "Who gives this bride away?" I said, "Her mother and I, Master Card, and First National Bank." All that money to give away daughters to other men who aren't nearly good enough so I can have grandchildren that are smarter than everyone else's.

Why would I pay through the nose all these years? Why would no cost be too great if it concerned my children? I guess it is because I don't understand anatomy very well. I think my nose is connected to my heart – which actually wouldn't be a bad idea because every time I sneezed it would clear my arteries, which would save me money. There I go being cheap again. Actually, I'm wired just like my Heavenly Father; it cost Him a lot to love His children.

In the Race of Life, We All Need a Pit Stop

After an elementary teacher taught a science lesson on magnets, she gave her students a quiz to see how much they had learned. One of the questions read, "My name starts with M. I have six letters and I pick up things. What am I?" Half the class answered with the six-letter word mother.

Thank goodness God made mothers because mothers not only pick up things; they also pick us up. Who is the first person you think about when you fall down and go boom? Chances are it is your mother.

God had a great idea when he invented mothers. I have the old fashioned kind of mom. She still thinks that the kitchen is for something other than resale value. The breakfast I had growing up was a little like heaven – biscuits, cream gravy, bacon, and sausage – a cholesterol picnic. It was wonderful. Mom cooked from scratch and made clothes from scratch.

But there were also some unpleasant times in my childhood. I guess everyone has his or her dysfunctions. It was those times when Mom made me go to Cloth World or Cloth Barn or City of Cloth. These stores were always off by themselves, no place to go or run to, just mom and me in Cloth Hell. I felt so feminine. It was traumatic. I've since joined a group called Adult Children of Seamstresses Anonymous and am actually two steps away from walking through Cloth World without wetting my pants.

Moms are different now. They don't have as much time to spend with their children. It starts early. They get only one night in a hospital to have a baby. Now I know what HMO stands for – Hurry Mothers Out. I guess moms have to work harder than ever.

We know evolution isn't true; otherwise, why do mothers still have only two hands and politicians only one mouth?

Being a mother is tough. You know you're a mother when you understand everything the family dog says, or when you have a reoccurring dream that you are the agitator of the washing machine and you're off balance. You know you're a mother when one of your biggest fears is that there will be carpooling in heaven, or when you think Barney is a real person.

And of course kids get into as much trouble as ever. One kid said his mother's prayer for him every night was, "Thank God he's in bed."

I heard about a mother who finished a backbreaking job of stripping the kitchen floor and re-waxing it for Christmas. She heard her husband say, "Kids, your mother has worked hard on this floor. See how nice and clean it looks? I want you to be careful because anyone who spills anything on the floor has to clean it up first, go to the spare room, close the door, and stay there by yourself for an hour." When the mother heard this decree, she spilled coffee on the floor, cleaned it up, and ran to the room. No one saw her for an hour.

Motherhood is filled with frustration, difficulty, and challenges, but eventually they move out.

Mothers want the best for their children. A guy told his buddy that he had given up on dating. The friend asked, "What's wrong? Can't find anyone good enough for you?" He responded, "No, I can't find anyone good enough for my mother."

Of course, you can never forget your loyalty to your mom. While standing at attention during a parade, a private started to wave at a woman in the audience. The drill sergeant sternly warned the private, "Jones, don't ever do that again!" A few minutes later, however, the private waved again. The sergeant became livid at Jones and pointed out the dangers of disobeying a superior officer and shouted a few severe threats. Jones still seemed remorseless. The sergeant said, "Boy, aren't you afraid of me and what I could do to you?" Jones replied, "Oh, yes, sir, but you don't know my mother; I've got to wave at her." That private is a lot like a police recruit who was asked during the exam, "What would you do if you had to arrest your own mother?" The recruit answered, "I'd call for backup."

Mother's aren't perfect. They sometimes talk a little too much. A couple of kids went to their father with a question. He said, "Go ask your mother." The children responded, "We don't want to know that much."

Life isn't as scary with a mom around. It's like the story of the little boy who was in first grade. He strutted in front of his classmates and proclaimed, "When I grow up, I'm going to be a lion tamer. I'll have lots of fierce lions and when I walk in the cage, they will roar." He paused a moment and looked at his classmates' faces and then added, "Of course, I'll have my mother with me."

There is just something about having your mom with you. If life is like a grueling race, then time with mom is like a pit stop. It is a time of refreshment. Even my girls, who have babies of their own, still call home, and it's evident they just need their mom. The race is hard and they need a pit stop. When I fly through Dallas, I like to stop at Mom's and just spend a little time, have a great breakfast, and even take her to Cloth World.

A little boy was in the Easter play. He was fortunate to have the part of Jesus and one of his lines was, "I am the light of the world." He got to that line and forgot it. His mother just had to help. You know how mothers are. She moved out of the audience and stood in front so she could help him. He looked at his mother and she mouthed the words, "I am the light of the world." He smiled at his mother, turned to the audience, and said, "My mother is the light of the world."

Mothers may not be the light of the world, but they definitely brighten it up – probably because they reflect so much of God's love.

Family Trips

We took many family trips. The other day I was thinking about root canals, leprosy, IRS audits, and family trips. I think it was Churchill who said, "We have fought in the valleys, by the rivers, and on the mountain." That sounds a lot like some of our family trips.

First of all, I have three daughters. Now the reason I have three daughters is I lied when Penny and I were dating. She asked if I loved the mall, and I said, "Oh yes, I love the mall. It is wonderful just to watch you shop." God was listening, and he turned to the birth angel and said, "Charles is lying. We need to teach him a lesson. Give him three girls so he will spend his life at the mall."

So not only do I go to the mall a lot, but I also live in a girls' dorm. We have so much hair spray in our house that everything sticks in mid air. The only thing male in my house is the mailbox. Sometimes when I need some male companionship, I confess I have gone out and actually talked to the mailbox. I'm sure one day I will die of pantyhose strangulation.

I did pretty well around the house, but trips were difficult. First you have to understand male-female differences. You see, a man starts a trip thinking, "How many miles can I make in one day?" A woman is thinking, "How many times can I stop in one day?"

A woman just doesn't understand competition. Penny will say, "Let's stop at the next rest area," and I'll say, "Not until I pass that Ford." She says, "What Ford?" "The one that passed me thirty minutes ago that I've been trying to catch." A woman just can't understand how a man *can't relax* at a rest stop because he sees all those cars racing by that he spent the last two hours passing. It's downright discouraging.

Then you add children to the trip. There is something about two adults and three children in a metal cylinder for 1,000 miles that brings out the devil in everyone. Any trip over 100 miles can help you understand why some animals eat their young. Kids say things like, "She is breathing my air," or "Her foot is on my side." After the ten-minute quiet game, you invent counting games. Two hours into the trip you have counted cows, signs, letters in signs, eighteen-wheelers who honk and don't honk, Volkswagens, and black Volkswagens (they count more than anything else). By now you have told the kids to count on being murdered if you have to correct them one more time.

Then your wife says, "We appear to be lost." Of course a man is never lost. He is just temporarily misplaced. The word "lost" to men means to drive faster. A man thinks God put something inside his head like a heat-seeking device, and if he will just drive faster he will find what he is looking for. That's why a man will go thirsty, his wife will go hungry, and the children will wet their pants, but he will never stop to ask for directions although he is as lost as a ball in tall weeds.

Well, I could go on and tell you about the time we left Penny at the rest stop, but you get the picture. Family trips – they were awful. I wonder why I miss them so much.

Ever Make Mistakes?

Our church in Dallas was very large and easy to get lost in. After church, our family always met on the second floor of one building. On one particular Sunday we were supposed to go out to eat with some couples, and everyone was going to meet at the same place. We all showed up at the appropriate time except my teenaged daughter, Angela. She was about thirteen and she wasn't there. (At the time I didn't realize she wouldn't be there for the next six years.) We waited ten minutes – still not there. Finally, people were getting antsy and I was getting embarrassed. One couple said, "We'll go to the restaurant and save a place because it's going to get crowded." Another couple said, "We know you don't know the way to the restaurant, so we'll stay and you can follow us." I said, "Thank you for going and saving a table. Thank you for staying." Meanwhile, even though I was acting so appreciative, I was getting angry.

Finally, fifteen minutes late, Angela came be-bopping up, like teenagers do, and said, "Hey, Dad, what's happening?" At this point I was about boiling. Those of us who work on a church staff learn to develop the fine art of hollering with our mouths closed. I'm pretty good at that. I said, with my teeth clenched, "Angela, where have you been?" She said, "I've been in Sunday School." "No you haven't; you're fifteen minutes late. Where have you been for the last fifteen minutes?" "Daddy, calm down, I lost my shoes." "You did WHAT?" "I lost my shoes." "Where?" "I lost my shoes in Sunday School." "How could you lose your shoes in Sunday School?" She said, "Daddy, I'm going to tell you. It's an all-girls class, and our Sunday shoes are uncomfortable, so we always take them off and put them in the corner, and after Sunday School we put them back on. Today the boys somehow snuck into our room during break time, stole the shoes, and took them down the hall. It took us fifteen minutes to find our shoes."

After she finished her story, I came out with one of those gems I like to call "parental stupidisms." They are the things parents say to kids that make no sense whatsoever but make the parents feel better. All parents do this. It's like when you say to your kid, "If you fall out of that tree and break your leg, don't come running to me." I said, "Angela, don't you ever take your shoes off again as long as you live." It made no sense, but it did make me feel better.

Anyway, we got into the car and headed for the restaurant. The McCullochs were in front of us because I didn't know the way. One of their kids went with us, and one of our kids went with them. The McCullochs were driving a gray Buick, and I was following them to the restaurant. Everybody was laughing and having a good time except Daddy. He was "wrought." Angela, grrr, shoes, grrr, late, grrr; just grrr. All of a sudden, in the middle of everybody's laughter, somebody said, "Did the McCullochs get a new car?" The McCulloch kid, in the back, jumped up and said, "Did we get a new car?" – like they might have traded it in during Sunday School. I started to look closely at the car ahead of us and then somebody said, "I think that's a Cadillac." And the McCulloch kid said, "Did we get a Cadillac?" And then I think my wife said, "I don't think that's the McCulloch's car." And the McCulloch kid said, "That's not our car."

Then the whole car was totally quiet. Everybody knew not to say a word or the guy driving might explode. But Breanne, who was only about seven at the time and didn't know any better, started laughing and said, "Isn't this funny? Angela lost her shoes, but Daddy lost a whole car." Well, at that point everybody broke up laughing, and I pulled off the road because I didn't know where I was going or whom I was following anyway. I turned to Angela and said, "I'm sorry, Honey. I hollered at you and acted ugly. Will you forgive me?" She said, "Sure, Dad, we all make mistakes."

All of us *do* make mistakes, don't we? Why don't we treat other's mistakes as we would like our mistakes treated? Sound familiar?

Do You Understand Me?

It's hard for kids to understand church. One little boy went to see a musical called "Mr. Salty." He loved the musical and he loved Mr. Salty. The next Sunday in church he got extremely angry and left the building. When his mother found him he had tears in his eyes and said, "I hate this church." "Why?" asked his mother. "They hate Salty and I love Salty." "What do you mean, Son?" "They were singing it over and over again in church." The new chorus in church was, "I Exalt Thee." But the boy understood "I hate Salty."

Kids also get their prayers mixed up. One kid prayed, "And forgive us our trash baskets as we forgive those who put trash in our baskets." Kids think concretely. Adults say one thing and kids hear whatever makes sense to them. Like the kid who prayed, "Give us this day our jelly bread." Or another that comes to mind is the kid who had trouble in his second grade class with Mrs. Murphy. When he tried to quote the scripture "Surely goodness and mercy will follow me all the days of my life," it came out, "Surely good Mrs. Murphy will follow me all the days of my life."

When we speak to children we must take time to communicate clearly to them. We have to learn to enter into the child's world. This is especially true when it comes to behavior. Parents will often tell a child what *not* to do, and the child will hear the instructions with good intentions to obey what the parent said, but will end up doing exactly what he wasn't supposed to do. Why? Was it the child's behavior or the parent's instruction? It was both. "He did what I said, my son, my good buddy. I said don't get dirty, so instead he got muddy."

One preacher's kid had to sit by himself in church since his mother was in the choir and his father was preaching. Every time his dad began to preach, the boy left his front row seat to go to the bathroom. Exasperated, his dad told him, "I don't want to see you go to the bathroom in church today. Do you understand me?" "Yes," said the boy.

The boy understood his father didn't want to *see* him go to the bathroom. In the child's mind, going to the bathroom wasn't the problem, seeing him go was the problem. So in the middle of the service, he had to go. He crawled under the pews all the way to the end so his dad wouldn't *see* him. His dad saw a lot of confused faces as the boy crawled through the pews to the exit. The boy thought he was doing exactly what his dad wanted him to do, and of course his dad thought it was the worst thing he could have done.

I have a pastor friend whose son was supposed to care for the family dog. The boy continually left the back gate open, and the dog would get out. Finally the pastor had reached his limit. He told his son, "If you let the dog out one more time, when I get home, I'm going to burn your britches." Sure enough the kid left the gate open and the dog got out. Keep in mind this was a small town and everyone knew where the pastor lived. His mother looked out the kitchen window and saw her son taking all his clothes off as he stood in front of a barrel of water. Embarrassed and shocked she ran outside. "What are you doing?" The boy replied, "Dad said if I let the dog out one more time he was going to burn my britches. These are my favorite britches so I'm putting them in this barrel of water so they will be so wet they won't burn."

Why would I spend so much time talking about children and church? Most adults in church don't understand what we're talking about either. You say one thing and they hear another. Communicate on a child's level, and you'll be surprised how many adults will also understand.

Are We Having Fun Yet?

As our girls were growing up, I spent father/daughter time with each one by taking them individually on a trip with me. They picked the destination and the restaurants. One year Breanne chose Orlando, home of Disney World. Our hotel was right by McDonald's. Needless to say, we had fourteen meals at McDonald's that week. I was soon called McCharles. At Disney World, I was able to watch the interaction between parents and their children and noticed that most of the kids weren't having any fun at this place built for kids. I saw a man dragging his kid while telling him, "You're going to see Mickey Mouse." The kid said, "But I don't like Mickey Mouse." The father countered, "I've driven 677 miles, and you're going to see Mickey Mouse." Other children were hurried from ride to ride; parents were trying to get the best dollar per ride ratio. They figured they had paid $50 and they needed to ride at least thirty rides. Of course that logic made the kids miserable. Here I was at the place made for fun, and most kids weren't having any.

Let me ask you something. Have you had any fun lately? I live in a state where people flock to casinos. Why? Do they go to make money? I don't think so, I doubt if their IQ Test came back negative. They are looking for fun. I guess the biggest compliment we received as a family was from our niece. She stayed with us for a weekend and said, "I like to stay at Uncle Charles and Aunt Penny's house. It's the laughing house." She meant that it was a place where people liked to have fun.

It wasn't always that way. I realized at one point in my life that I was against just about everything. My kids would ask, "Can we do that?" I'd say, "No it's too expensive." "Can we do this?" "No, we're Christians." "Well, how about that?" "No, it's Sunday." My kids would finally ask, "Well, what can we do?" "Nothing," I would say, "You can't do anything that's fun. You have to be miserable the rest of your life, just like me."

Sadly, the worst day of the week was Sunday. It is incredible what happens on Sundays. People scream at each other. They holler and say, "You have twenty-eight seconds to eat those Fruit Loops; we have to go to church. Praise Jesus." You know how it is when you're trying to get the family ready for church. You have to get everyone dressed and teeth brushed. Dads are what I call "heavenly honkers." The men go out to the car and honk, honk, honk, "We have to go, we're late!" We don't think about helping. We just honk and holler.

It was the same way when I grew up. We got in the car, slammed the door, and everyone was in a bad mood. We looked more steamed than redeemed. Then we drove by the heathen's house. You know the heathens. The father is in his undershirt drinking a Miller Lite and playing softball with the kids. Everyone is laughing and having fun. And in the car it's miserable. Just about that time my Dad sees the heathens and he says, "Look at those heathens out there, they don't know the joy of Jesus." My brothers and I made a commitment in the backseat of our car that we would be heathens when we grew up. They seemed to be the only ones having fun. It didn't get any better when we arrived at church. It seemed like someone was always disciplining me for running in God's house or even in His yard.

One time our family decided to get up thirty minutes early to get ready for church just to see if we could lighten the stress. We were ready for church early, and no one knew what to do. It had never happened before in our family and probably never happened in the history of Christendom.

Jesus had fun. The first public event He went to was a party (a wedding feast in Cana). He didn't share the four spiritual laws with anyone, He just had fun. My kids are grown now, and we talk about what they remember as children. They don't remember a single speech I delivered although I had some good ones. What they do remember is that we had fun.

This Sunday, why don't you try it? Start things a little earlier, and on the way home from church you be the one to suggest having some fun. Say something like, "Why don't we stop and get a pizza and play some video games?" Your family will think you're on drugs, or snorting Sweet 'N

Low. They may think they should put Dad into some treatment program. Or maybe they will think people who go to church have fun. Or better yet, they might go to church someday and take their family.

5

M&M (Miscellaneous Motivation)

Being cool is realizing you're not so hot. I'm not okay, you're not okay, and that's okay as long as we don't stay that way. This chapter motivates us in the areas of leading, relating, and even praying. It actually starts with your big toe, but it will gradually include all of you.

Bite Your Own Big Toe

Have you ever thought someone was a snob because he didn't speak to you, but later you found out that he had just heard some tragic news? He wasn't being a jerk, he was just in shock. Often, we don't know people's motives or their background, and we make a premature judgment which gets us into trouble.

Like the old man who took his ugly dog for his regular Sunday walk in the park. He sat on the park bench while his dog played at his feet. They weren't bothering anyone. Soon a younger man appeared with his dog. Both the young man and his dog had a mean, bulldog-type look on their faces. They were looking for a fight. The man and his bulldog began taunting the little old man and his ugly dog. The younger man commanded his dog, "Spike!" and pointed in the ugly dog's direction. The little old man calmly addressed the aggressor, "I wouldn't do that if I were you." Irritated by the old man's comment, the young man commanded Spike to attack the frail-looking mutt. The old man reiterated, "I wouldn't do that!" As the battle raged in cartoon fashion (lots of barking, dust flying and dogs running in circles), the result was unexpected. Spike lay defeated, torn to pieces by the ugly canine. His humbled master said to the old man, "What kind of dog is that?" to which the codger replied, "Well, before I cut off his tail and painted him yellow, he was an alligator!"

When we see things from our point of view only, we tend to antagonize instead of harmonize. Such myopia can lead to disaster because we all have a little alligator in us. It's simply a matter of perspective. A kid was being interviewed for a job at the movie theater. The man interviewing asked, "Now, son, what would you do if we had a fire at the theater?" The kid answered, "Don't you worry. I'd get out all right." He was looking at it from his point of view. The manager was asking how he would help others. If we're not careful, we see things only from our point of view.

A chicken and an elephant were locked in a cage together. The chicken turned to the elephant and said, "We need to set a few ground rules. First, let's not step on each other." The chicken was looking at it from his point of view. Our chicken point of view affects our relationship with others. Our tendency is to want to straighten people out for our own benefit. If you think straightening people out is your job, I suggest you become a funeral director. That way when you straighten them out, they'll stay straightened out.

Remember, God is the construction manager of people's lives, not you. Have you ever gone through a construction area and seen a sign that says, "Slow, Men Working"? That's absolutely right; there are slow men working. I thought about that sign the other day. We should put up a sign that says, "Slow, God Working." God works slowly. I don't think he wears a watch. To him a minute is like a million years. So let's put two signs in our minds that say, "Slow, God Working" and "Danger! Keep Out."

A football player decided he wanted to be a wrestler. The coach said he didn't think he would be any good at it because he didn't have any wrestling skills. But the kid was determined. His technique was awful, but he ended up at the state finals. He had to wrestle last year's state champion. The Champ was just killing him. It was so bad, the coach buried his head in his hands. All of a sudden a huge cheer came from the crowd, and the coach looked up. The kid had won the match. He asked, "How did you do that? One second you're losing and the next you win." The kid said, "He had me in some sort of position and I didn't know what to do. The only thing I could see was a big toe. So I bit the toe as hard as I could. Coach you won't believe what you can do when you bite your own big toe."

The truth is, we don't want to be stepped on, but often we're not careful about whom *we* step on. So the next time you feel like straightening someone out, go ahead and act like an alligator. Only this time, bite your own big toe.

I Feel Your Pain

When a first grader fell on the ice coming into church, the pastor tried to comfort him. "Remember, big boys don't cry." "Cry?" he replied, "I'm going to sue."

Do we live in a world where people would rather have money than comfort? Maybe, but we also know that at times we prefer comfort. Are we too selfish to give comfort? When bus station employees were having a hard time keeping their door closed, they placed a sign on the door: "Please close the door for the comfort of others." However, the door still stayed open most of the day. The next day they put up another sign that read, "Please close the door for your own personal comfort." That day the door stayed closed.

Most of us would like to comfort others, but we just don't know how. Let's say you have a friend with a terrible toothache. He calls and says, "My tooth really hurts. Will you come over and just be with me and give me some comfort?" During your visit, you want to help him, but without thinking you blurt out, "I know you're in a lot of pain but there's a *reason* why you're in this mess. I have just one question. Are you brushing after every meal?" Your friend replies, "I'm hurting so badly, I don't even want to think about it right now." But you press on, "Are you flossing? I just happened to be in your bathroom, and I didn't see any dental floss. I can tell that you're not flossing. No wonder you're in pain. You ought to be in pain. Someone like you who never flosses..." Your friend responds, "I did floss. I used a shoestring. Go away, I'm hurting." You continue to try to "comfort" him. "How about regular checkups? Have you had your teeth cleaned? When was the last time you went to the dentist?" Soon your presence is more of a nuisance than a blessing.

It may sound absurd, but that's what we do when people suffer from spiritual pain. "When was the last time you were in church? I haven't seen you there; no wonder you're hurting. God's gonna get you." They want to reply, "Oh shut-up. Why did I share my pain with you? I knew you were a self-righteous guy. You come over here and tell me what's wrong with me, but all I needed was comfort." Yet we continue with our barrage.

So how do you help someone who is in physical pain? You might offer some practical help, "Can I go to the drugstore and get you anything? Do you need some Tylenol, or how about some Numbs-it? Maybe you'd like to see a movie to help take your mind off the toothache. Maybe I can rub your feet. Maybe that will help you forget about your toothache. Whatever you want me to do, I'll do it." Your goal is to help your friend deal with the pain and then, ultimately, to get him to a dentist. The dentist can do what you cannot, which is cure the problem rather than the symptoms.

We are not God no matter what Shirley MacLaine says. Theologically speaking, we're not the dentist. We cannot solve the real problem, but we are friends of God, who can. When we show genuine care for our hurting friends, they begin to trust us, and then they'll be more open to a visit to the dentist. After the pain subsides, they may listen to our lecture on tooth care, but not before. They need comfort before they need counsel.

In the sheep country of New Mexico, shepherds were losing lots of lambs in winter time. The problem was, the ewes would take their lambs out to graze late in the day, and when it started to snow, the temperature would drop below freezing. But the ewes were unaware of the danger to the lambs and would continue to graze, and soon the lambs would freeze to death. The shepherds realized that the reason the ewes were unaware of the danger was that they were covered with so much thick wool they didn't feel the drop in temperature. The shepherds had a unique solution. They sheared the top of the ewes' heads so, when the weather changed, they felt it and headed back to the barn, and the lambs followed them to safety.

The first step in helping others is to feel what they are feeling. That's the essence of comfort. That's what gets the sheep to the barn and people to the shepherd.

I Can See Clearly Now

I wear contact lenses. Without them I would need a seeing-eye dog. When the optometrist asks me to read the chart on the wall I always respond with, "What wall?" Recently I lost my contacts and needed a new pair quickly. The last time I ordered contacts it took forever to get them so I put a rush on this order. The saleslady said it would take six days for delivery. I told her, "You don't understand. I'm really in a hurry. Six days, surely it can't take six days? I'll do whatever it takes to speed up the process. Why does it take six days?" She said, "We don't make them here. They are shipped to us." I said, "The mail takes three days at the most." She said, "You don't seem to understand. We have to mail the prescription to the manufacturer and then they mail the contacts back, so it takes six days in all." I said, "Okay, I understand that. Let's just do this. I have a little cash here. I'll pay you for the long distance phone call and you can call and give the manufacturer the prescription for my contacts. Or even better than that, I'll give you more cash and after you call them, they can overnight them back. This is the twentieth century. Then I can come here tomorrow afternoon and pick them up." "Well, you couldn't pick them up tomorrow because the lab assistant must look at them before you can have them in order to be sure they are okay." "Well, after the lab looks at them, then you could call me and I'll come get them." She said,

"I'm sorry, but I believe it takes six days." Finally I said, "Is there a manager here?" "Yes, he's here." "May I talk to him?"

So the manager comes out and I say, "Sir, I'd like to get my contacts and I understand it takes six days." He said, "That's right. It does take six days." I said, "I told this lady here that I am willing to pay for a long distance phone call and an overnight express service fee, whatever it takes to get them here. Can you do that for me?" "Oh sure," he said, "I can do that."

The next day I called and was told, "Your contacts are not here yet." The next day they still weren't there. The next day I had to go out of town but when I returned on the sixth day I decided to go back to see them again. Well, actually not to *see* them but maybe to touch them since I didn't have any contacts and I couldn't see very well. I was ready to touch them right upside the head. I asked, "Where are my contacts?" The lady said, "Well, it takes six days." I said, "This *is* the sixth day. Besides that I thought the manager was going to help me get them here earlier." The lady said, "Well he must have forgotten." I said, "Are my contacts here now?" She said, "I don't know. We haven't checked the mail yet." "Could you check the mail?" She said, "Well, that's the manager's job." "Is the manager here?" "Not yet." Just then the manager walked in. I said, "Sir, is the mail here?" He said, "Oh, I forgot to check the mail. I'll be right back." He leaves and comes back with the mail, and my contacts are in the mail. "Here are your contacts, Dr. Lowery." "Great! Thank you." Then I remembered that they said that the lab assistant had to check my contacts. I knew better but before I thought I said, "I can take them now, right? The lab assistant doesn't really have to look at these, does she?" As I started to leave the lady said, "Oh yes, that's right. The lab assistant has to look at them." So I said, "Then I'll wait. Get the lab assistant." She hesitated and then said, "I hate to tell you this, but the lab assistant is home sick today. But if you promise not to wear these, you can take them home but bring them back tomorrow." I said, "I promise I will not wear these contacts." I backed out of the door repeating, "I promise I won't wear these contacts until I get back to the office." Then I ran as fast as I could.

I was seething when I got back to the office. I was so angry I was thinking, "God, if you can just send an earthquake and wipe them out, that would be great with me." God spoke back to me. Now God doesn't talk to me audibly. I'm not in TV evangelism. I never understood that anyway. I mean, if God lives inside of me, why would He go outside to talk to me? That would be like my kids being inside the house and my going outside and hollering through the window to see if they can hear me. No, I would just talk to them on the inside. That's the way God talks to me. Anyway, He said, "Charles, you're angry, aren't you?" I said, "Yes, I am." He said, "Why is that, Charles?" I replied, "Because those people are incompetent and stupid. There's no way it should take six days to get a pair of contacts." Then I heard God say, "Charles, don't hold it against *them* for being incompetent and stupid, and I won't hold it against *you* for being incompetent and stupid. Compared to me, Charles, you don't get a lot accomplished in six days either. I created the world in six days. What have you accomplished in your last six days?" I responded, "God, I think I see. I mean, I really see."

You're an Original: Don't Be a Carbon Copy

God loves you and has a plan for your life. The problem is, other people who don't love you also have a plan for your life. It's pretty tough being what God designed you to be – especially among people who seem to think God made all of us as divine duplicates.

When my wife and I were first dating, we would often eat with her parents. Her father is one of those serious type guys – you know, the ones with the plastic pocket protector with all the pencils in order. He would ask scientific questions at the dinner table, which made me nervous. I was a preacher's kid. I was used to knock-knock jokes at the dinner table.

When Penny and I got married, he visited our house. He just walked around taking notes. Finally he said, "Charles, you have some things that need to be fixed. Get your toolbox." Well, I didn't have a toolbox – I had super glue, duct tape, and WD-40. If I couldn't tape it, glue it, or spray it then I figured God didn't want it fixed. I wouldn't know what to do with a toolbox. I had a mechanical bypass very early in life. I don't remember the surgery, but I have no mechanical ability. I went to the school for the mechanically challenged, but that didn't help.

What to do? I'll fake it so my father-in-law will approve of me. I told him I'd get my toolbox and be right back. I borrowed a neighbor's toolbox. He said, "Let's get to work. I'll crawl under there and you hand me the tools." He hollered out, "Crescent." All I could find was a Craftsman so I handed him a Craftsman. He laughed, crawled out, and got a crescent. He hollered out, "Phillips." All I could find was a Craftsman so I handed him a Craftsman. He laughed, crawled out, and got a Phillips. It was a very long day pretending to be somebody I wasn't, just to get my father-in-law's approval.

Later, I realized that he was trying to be somebody he's not, just to get my approval. You see, I was always telling him jokes and one-liners and so he felt as if he had to be a funny guy as well. Unfortunately, he didn't know any jokes so he memorized "Humor in Uniform" out of the *Readers Digest*. They were awful. As you can imagine, our relationship was quite stressful. Remember this: good relationships are about to end when you have to pretend.

After a while I just couldn't take it anymore. I sat Pop down and told him about my mechanical bypass. He said, "Those jokes I tell aren't very funny, are they?" I said, "They are some of the worst I've heard." What a relief: it's out. We're different, and that's okay. Matter of fact, we have a great relationship. When he comes to our house he brings his own toolbox, and I have a list of things for him to fix. He goes around and fixes everything in the house, and all I do is walk around with him and tell him funny stories.

God made me unique. From reading this book, you know that I'm different. I can pretend to try to be like you, or I can just accept myself as God made me. Maybe I can even use a little humor to share some of God's truths. By the way, have you heard the one about...?

Arrows in the Back

A well-known politician, riding in a train, held up a five-dollar bill and said, "I'm going to throw this five-dollar bill out the window and make somebody happy." One of his ardent admirers suggested, "But, sir, why don't you throw five one-dollar bills out the window and make five people happy?" A member of the opposition, seated in a corner, growled, "Why don't *you* jump out and make everybody happy?"

The leader of a small country was bitterly disappointed that nobody used the newly-issued postage stamps bearing his portrait. He questioned his postmaster, who explained the stamps were not sticking. Seizing a stamp, the dictator licked it and stuck it onto an envelope. "Look!" he shouted. "It sticks perfectly!" The postmaster faltered for a moment, and then explained, "Well, sir, the truth is that the people have been spitting on the wrong side."

The truth is, whoever leads the pack gets arrows in the back. Critics are everywhere, even in church. They sit so far back in the church, by the time they hear anything, it's already a rumor. They weren't born again;

they were born against. At the beginning of every meeting you feel like calling on them for a word of criticism just to get it over with. Their favorite TV character is Oscar the Grouch on *Sesame Street*. Their faces look like Lamentations. They always have that "I'm in pain" look. Maybe it's the side effects of having an artificial heart.

I always try to be positive with my critics. I saw one last week and I told him, "If I had two more just like you, I'd be a happy man." He didn't know what to say. He said, "Charles, what are you talking about? I'm always criticizing you. Why would you be happy if you had two more like me?" I said, "Because now I have twenty like you. If I had only three, I would be a happy man!"

Someone has said that any fool can criticize, condemn, and complain, and most fools do. For every step forward, there is an equal and opposite criticism.

Many times as leaders, we feel as if our colors ought to be black and blue. The fact is, all leaders are criticized. Lincoln and Washington, two of our greatest Presidents, were constantly criticized. Churchill once received a standing ovation, and a lady commented how flattering it must be to receive that kind of applause. "Yes," he said, "but I also know that if it were my hanging, the crowd would be twice the size."

Every great endeavor has its critics. When Robert Fulton first showed off his new invention, the steamboat, skeptics were crowded on the bank yelling, "It'll never start! It'll never start!" It did. It started with a lot of clanking and groaning. As the steamboat made its way down the river, the skeptics were quiet for one minute. Then they started shouting, "It'll never stop! It'll never stop!"

How do you respond to criticism? One week I received a lot of criticism, and a staff member's wife said to me, "When I hear criticism I get a knot in my stomach." I'm just the opposite. When I hear criticism I want to give my critics a knot on their heads. Do you hit them or do you pray that they will fry in their own grease? What about setting clever traps for them – like the guy who was upset because his critic was always poking him in the chest. He decided to wire dynamite to his chest so that the next time his critic poked him, he would go up in smoke. That's not a good idea. Take the rocks thrown at you and build something. Don't be paranoid. Everybody's not out to get you. There is no coat that will insulate you from criticism. Remember that critics who try to whittle you down are only trying to reduce you to their size.

When dealing with critics, learn some lessons from the building of the Panama Canal. The builder of the Panama Canal was besieged with criticism. When asked how he was going to handle the critics, he said, "With the canal." Don't get sidetracked if you are on the right track. Stay positive. One football coach says that when you are run out of town, go to the head of the line and look as though you are leading a parade.

So remember, a critic a day probably means you're heading the right way, and arrows in the back mean you are still in front of the pack.

What If There Is No Cure?

What if the remedy doesn't work? I heard about a farmer whose chickens were dying. He called the agricultural agent and said, "I had 600 chickens and now I'm down to 300. They're all dying. What do I do?" The agent said, "You need to give them penicillin." A few days later he told the agent he was down to 150 chickens. "They are dying quickly. I need some more advice." The agent said, "Give them some castor oil twice a day. That ought to help." The farmer called back in a few days and said he was down to fifty chickens. The agent said, "This is what you do: give them aspirin twice a day." Two days later he told the agent all the chickens were dead. There was silence on the line. Then the agent said, "That's a shame. I have a lot more remedies to try."

We want to keep trying remedies, but some things can't be fixed. It was children's day at church, and a small girl got one of those big blue helium balloons. All of a sudden, it popped! The big balloon was nothing but a blob of rubber. Her face turned to gloom and then, as if something struck her, she picked up that glob of blue rubber and. again started cheerfully hopping and skipping as she ran to her daddy and said, "Here. Fix it."

What do you do when you can't fix it? You have to move from compassion to comfort. I believe there is a difference between compassion and comfort. Comfort is putting compassion into action. A little girl took first aid training. A few years later she burst into the house and said, "Mother, I saw a terrible accident and I used my first aid training." Mother asked her what she did. She said, "I saw a lot of blood so I sat down and put my head between my knees so I wouldn't pass out." Well, that wasn't very comforting. Compassion leads to comfort. Compassion leads to taking the initiative. Because Beethoven was deaf, he found conversation difficult. When he heard of the death of a friend's son, he hurried over to the house, overcome with grief. He had no words of comfort to offer, but he saw a piano in the room. For the next half-hour he played the piano, pouring out his emotions in the most eloquent way he could. After playing, he left. The friend later remarked that no one else's visit had meant so much. Beethoven did what he could.

A little boy was suddenly aware of the puddle between his feet and that the front of his pants was all wet. How could it have happened? Embarrassed, he wanted to die. The guys would never let him forget it; the girls would never speak to him again. "Please, dear God" he prayed. "I'm in big trouble here. I need help now." Suddenly a classmate named Suzie lost her grip on the goldfish bowl she was carrying. It tipped over, right in the boy's lap. "Thank you, dear God," he silently rejoiced. He pretended to be angry with Suzie and she then became the center of classroom scorn. He rushed to the office for a pair of dry gym shorts. After school the two were waiting for the bus. Suzie was standing off by herself, but he went up to her and whispered, "You did that on purpose, didn't you?" and Suzie whispered back, "I wet my pants once, too."

Comfort is not arguing about the facts but acknowledging the feeling. Comfort is being honest enough to say, "I don't understand it either, but I know God loves you." Comfort is doing what you can. Comfort is giving part of your heart instead of a piece of your mind. Comfort cares even when there appears to be no cure. So if you see me wet my pants, help me. Throw something wet at me. If there's nothing wet around, then wet your pants. It won't be comfortable for you, but it will be comfort to me.

Mental Hospitals, Superheroes, or Friends

Did you know that if you isolate yourself from other people, you are two to three times more likely to die an early death? You are more likely to contract terminal cancer if you are isolated from others. If you are divorced, separated, or widowed, you have a five- to ten-times greater chance of being hospitalized for mental disorders than if you are married. Some of you might be a little discouraged with your marriage, but focus on the positive; it's keeping you out of the mental hospital.

Living alone can make you crazy. You will go crazy and won't even realize it. For example, married people don't go crazy without realizing it because their mates will tell them, "You're crazy!"

There are several good ways to stay sane. You can go see a shrink and lie on a sofa and talk about your mother, you can get married (by the way, both are very expensive), or you can have friends. God said it isn't good to be alone. We need other people. Even when Simon was singing, "I am a rock, I am an island," he had Garfunkle singing back up. The Lone Ranger wouldn't have made it without Tonto. We need friends.

A football coach was having a very bad year. It got so bad that, when he confided to his wife, "'I feel that my dog is my only friend, but a man needs at least two friends", she bought him another dog.

We all need true friends – someone you can call to come get you if you arrive at the airport at one in the morning and your car won't start. We need friends who walk in when everyone else walks out.

A Los Angeles police officer took training in how to deal with snakebite victims. The trainer even taught the officers what to do if they were bitten by a snake but were unable to get medical attention. He explained in great detail that under extreme circumstances one would have to cut his or her skin with a sharp knife and suck out the venom by mouth. At that point the officer asked, "What happens if I get bitten on my behind?" After a long pause the instructor said, "Then you'll find out if you have any friends." When life hits you from behind, you need friends.

A good friend will do five things for you. The first is to bring *good cheer*. We need encouragement. We need to be told that the light at the end of the tunnel is not a train.

A good friend has a *listening ear*. Many people don't listen; they just reload waiting to tell you what you've done wrong. We don't always want answers; we want assurance. Sometimes we don't need solutions; we just need sympathy.

A good friend will often shed a *sensitive tear*. We need to be comforted. Comfort is the ability to stick it out without pointing it out. Kids understand comfort better than adults. Little Johnny was supposed to be home from school at a certain time each day. One day he was particularly late. When he came in his mother asked, "Where have you been?" He said, "I had to help a friend." "What happened?" asked his mother. "My friend fell down and started to cry." "And what did you do?" "I sat down and cried with him." That's comfort.

A good friend is not afraid to give us a *kick in the rear*. I need someone to remind me what the Nike commercial says – "Just Do It!"

And a good friend will speak the *truth without fear* – he will tell us the truth. A few years ago I had back problems, and my friend told me, "Your back is not your problem, Charles, it's your stomach. Your stomach is so big it's straining your back." First I was insulted and asked if he had been educated at pro-wrestling events. Then I realized he was right. I was getting bigger. I noticed it when I went out in my yellow rain coat and the people were running behind me hollering "Taxi." A friend will see through you, or in my case, around me, and also see you through. I lost weight, and now my back is fine because a friend wasn't afraid to tell me the truth.

Remember, good cheer, a listening ear, a sensitive tear, a kick in the rear, and truth without fear. That's what friends are for, and a true friend will know what you need because a friend is always near.

A little boy and his family moved often over a period of a few years. It's tough when you are in and out of different schools so often. One day when he was sitting at home in a melancholy mood, the boy asked his dad, "Who do you want to be, Superman or Batman?" Dad replied, "Well, Son, you know I'm kind of busy right now..." "Dad, come on. Who do you want to be, Superman or Batman?" "Well, Superman, Son. I want to be Superman." "Why, Dad? Why would you want to be Superman?" "Well, I don't know, Son. He can fly; that's why. Yeah, that's it; he can fly. I'd like to be Superman because he can fly." And Dad went about his business. The little boy continued, "Dad, aren't you going to ask me who I want to be?" So the Dad complied, "Okay, who do you want to be, Superman or Batman?" "I want to be Batman." The father said, "Good Son, that's good." The boy continued, "Dad, aren't you going to ask me why?" "Okay," the father sighed, "why do you want to be Batman?" "I want to be Batman because Batman has a friend." Dad stopped, turned around, and saw a tear in his son's eye. He asked, "Son, do you need a friend?" "Yeah," he said, "I need a friend more than I need Superman."

I suspect that some of you need a friend, and someone you know needs a friend. The best way to find a friend is to be a friend. Actually, you don't find friends; you recognize them. Be on the look out.

Leave It to Beaver

A college president friend of mine called and asked me, "Do you believe in free speech?" I said, "Yes." He said, "Good. Do you believe in education?" I said, "Yes." He said, "Good. I want you to make a free speech for education at my university." On this particular occasion I agreed.

One of the college students picked me up at the airport. His car was a cross between an old clunker and a bicycle. I knew I was in trouble when the student asked me not only to buckle my seatbelt but also to put on a helmet. He said we would have to reach top speed in order to merge onto the interstate.

As we left the airport for the university, I heard a loud "boom!" It sounded like a truck backfiring. The student said, "Oh, man, that's my car." He pulled over and as the car died he asked me what to do. I said, "I don't know. In times like these, guys are supposed to raise the hood and look inside." That's what we did. Then he asked, "What do we do now?" I said, "I don't know. If spraying WD-40 doesn't work, then I don't have a clue. I suggest we try to find a phone." The next exit with a service station was a long way away, so I got out my suitcase and put on my sneakers. I was dressed to give a speech so now I had on a nice suit and tie with sneakers. It was the "dork" look.

We walked down the road and as we got to the exit, I realized that this was not a safe area of town. It made me nervous. The traffic light didn't say "walk" and "don't walk" it said "run for your life." The convenience store had a metal detector. I knew this was going to be tough. Even the Avon lady probably had a pimp. It looked as if we could walk another three blocks without ever leaving the scene of a crime. No policemen were at the doughnut shop.

We found a store with a telephone outside the door. When the telephone area code is 911, you know it's not a good part of town. Several guys were standing around the telephone and I looked for the one who looked as if he had been out of the prison release program the longest. There wasn't much of a choice. I finally asked one man, "Does that telephone work?" He said, "You can call out, but no one can call in." I was trying to make conversation hoping this guy might eventually help me. I asked, "Why is that?" trying to be nice. He said, "Beaver..." I don't know why he called me Beaver. Maybe it was from *Leave it to Beaver*. Maybe I looked like a beaver. I don't know, but he said "Beaver," and I answered to that. I would have answered to anything under those circumstances. "Beaver," he said, "the reason no one can call in is because they sell drugs here." I thought I would get the best possible spin on this so I said, "Well, do you have a drug store here? Maybe there is a hospital close by. Maybe I can get a cab." He looked at me and said, "Beaver, they sell illegal drugs here." I asked, "Is there any chance of getting a cab to come out here?" He said, "Beaver, pizza isn't even delivered to this part of town."

It was an interesting hour as we slowly watched the graffiti change colors in the sunset. I knew that we would eventually be rescued and we were. I also realized that I liked the guy who looked like he was from the release program and he probably liked me too. As I left, I wondered what he felt like knowing that he would probably never be rescued in this world. I also thought that maybe I should wear sneakers more often than dress shoes, and maybe I should visit more places where people need help rather than just going to places where I feel welcome.

Free Ties

My oldest daughter went to a private university. Private universities don't charge tuition. They just say, "Send all the money you have." And they had taken all I had.

During these college days, I had a speaking engagement and was hoping for a good honorarium to help me pay for the tuition. But when my host picked me up, he had "stingy" written all across his forehead. When I got off the plane, I immediately knew I was in trouble because my host said, "I parked in remote parking," as I stood there holding a suitcase in each hand. Remote parking was about a mile away. He saved about seventy-five cents. We carried the luggage all the way to the car and drove to the motel. If I am speaking for more than one day, I usually rent a car. I was going to be there for three days, so I asked about a rental car. This guy told me he wanted to save some money and just to call him when I needed to go somewhere and he'd take me.

He dropped me off at Joe's Motel/Bait Shop/Chinese Food & Dry Cleaners, one of those all-in-one places. In the good motels, the glass will break if you drop it and the soap will bounce. In a bad motel, the soap will break and the glass will bounce. Also, the bolted down TV, a required damage deposit, and the restaurant's taking Blue Cross-Blue Shield are good signs of a bad motel. I was trying to be spiritual and content at Joe's. If I wanted to go out I had to call for a ride, and if we ate out it was in the car.

We had a great conference. Many people came and responded well to my messages. Ironically, my relationship with the host got worse. Thursday morning he came by as I was checking out. He said (as he looked at the bill), "There are some personal phone calls here on the bill, and you wouldn't want the church to pay for those." I wanted to say, "You jerk! Those are calls to you to pick me up because you're too stingy to rent a car." But I was trying to be spiritual. I paid for the calls. Again we parked in remote parking, and I walked back to the airport. By this time, I was pretty ticked off and started to pray about it as I boarded the plane. The honorarium check was pitiful. He'd taken out all the expenses, and I was down to almost nothing for three days of work. This guy would have asked for a separate check at the Last Supper. I started to complain to God, "This is why I don't like to speak to churches in the first place!" And God spoke to me. By then we were about 31,000 feet in the air and closer to the home office, so I heard God quite well. He said, "Shut up! That guy was a jerk and stingy but he is not the only middleman I have. I can take care of you. Be cool, drink a Diet Coke, and relax." So I just let it go.

When I got to the office, a letter was waiting for me from a church where I'd been about two months earlier. Included was a check and a note that said, "After you left, there was such a good response to your messages we made and sold tapes. Here's the money." It was a large check, more than I thought I'd get at the other place.

Why worry about stuff like this? God is loaded. He has it all. Yet so many times we want to grab for what we think we need and all the while,

God wants to give us what He wants us to have. Amazing things happen when we depend on Him.

I went on a clothes fast last year. I had become an ad-aholic. If there was a 66% off sale, I was there. But then I was nominated for the VISA Hall of Fame and knew that things were getting out of control. So I stopped buying clothes, including ties. After a few months, an amazing thing happened. I would show up to a speaking engagement and in my motel room would be a tie. Who gives ties? I usually get Diet Coke and Snickers as a welcome gift, but ties? It was as if God were saying, "You're looking a little sloppy; I'll get you some new ties." I quit speaking for churches and businesses. Oh, I still go to those places, but I'm speaking for God. He pays better and gives free ties.

The Gospel According to Pooh

One Thursday morning, before God had turned on the lights, I was up. I had procrastinated on my message preparation. I believe like the old country preacher that procrastination is one of the main doctrines of the church. Some tasks have to be put off many times before they slip your mind completely. By Thursday, the Noon Business Lunch had completely slipped my mind. I realized that I was totally unprepared to address this luncheon.

I had just started to study when I heard the sound of little feet. My youngest, Breanne, who was four at the time, walked into the room. Have you ever noticed that God made kids backwards when it's time for them to get up? When you want them up, they're as responsive as church members at offering time. And when you don't want them to get up, they are like church members at benediction. I couldn't believe Breanne was up so early. She sat right down on my study materials.

The first step in child rearing is to master the hand-off – hand off to your wife as soon as possible. She gave birth to her; surely she'll know what to do with her. I suggested to Breanne that she go get in bed with Mom. "No," she said. "No" is usually the answer from a four-year-old because that is the word she has heard five zillion times. She has probably never heard the word "yes." Adults are good at saying "no," but bad at responding to "no." I said, "No? What do you mean No? It is the middle of the night, and everyone is supposed to be in bed." She asked, "Why aren't you in bed?" Kids quickly spot the obvious.

It's like the kid who toured the FBI headquarters and was shown the pictures of the ten most wanted men. He asked, "Why didn't you keep them when you took their picture?"

I told Breanne that I had to get up early to study so that I could speak at noon. She said, "Mother always tells Angela and Kasey they have to do their homework before they go to bed. You're going to be in big trouble." Even four-year-olds are good at pointing out other people's sins.

She was still sitting on the notes, offering to help me study, but I told her she couldn't even read yet. She said, "I know some jokes." She'd heard me speak before. She asked me what John the Baptist and Kermit the Frog had in common. I told her I didn't know. She said they have the same middle name. I smiled. She knew I was loosening up to the idea of her helping me. She had seen me work a crowd and now she was working me.

Then she said, "I have a great idea. Mom said you would watch *Winnie the Pooh* with me." "Did she say I would watch it at 4:00 in the morning?" "She said you would watch it with me when you had time, and it looks like we both have time and no one will bother us." It appeared that it was time to get spiritual. It was time to pull God out and get out of this. I said, "Daddy has a lunch meeting where I tell people about God, and if I don't study I won't have anything to tell them. So you go to bed and I'll study so people can hear about God." She said, "I have a better idea. You watch *Winnie the Pooh* with me, and you'll see that he is a lot like God. He listens to the children and spends time with them. He teaches them to do right. So you watch the video with me, and I'll let you take it with you and you can show the people the tape and tell them that's how God wants them to act." She was a little ahead of her time, videos and sermons, and I wish I could tell you that I had enough fortitude to play *Winnie the Pooh* to the business lunch, but I did tell them about Pooh and what I had learned.

That night when Breanne said her prayers she thanked God for Winnie the Pooh and, "Oh yeah, my dad." That night I felt I was in pretty good company. I also learned that if you can't relate God to the world people live in, you might not be communicating at all.

What about Bob?

Every church has a few. When we see them we think of that little "Family of God" chorus but change the words to, "I'm surprised you're a part of the family of God." God made them fearfully and wonderfully weird. They have the amazing ability to suck the joy right out of the ministry. They're a few French fries short of a Happy Meal; they're missing a few buttons on the remote. You know what I mean. The porch light is on but no one is home.

They even look a little funny. They must shop at "Nerds R Us." There is always something unbuttoned, undone, unzipped, or untucked. They are the Dagwoods of Simpletown.

When I see them I want to ask, "Where are Mo, Larry, and Curly?" They seem so inappropriate at times. They are usually standing when they are supposed to be sitting or talking when they are supposed to be quiet. They aren't cool, quick, or articulate like us. They aren't the sharpest knives in the drawer.

They wait until everyone is gone and never give up because they want to talk to you. They probably want to hug you. And there is always one who zeroes in on you; you are his hero, his idol, and the person he wants to spend as much time with as he can.

They are there after every service, waiting to tell you things you already know. Don't they remember they have already told you twice? They act as if just telling you will get them through. They irritate you, and you mumble under your breath when you see them coming. You try to avoid them. If they come down the center, you head for the right side. You develop plays to get around them, even find blockers to make sure your play works.

Let's be honest. Sometimes you're just rude. You blow them off because your time is too valuable. You know they are hurt but you do it anyway. You say something that cuts them off, or you embarrass them with your quick wit and it hurts but it works. Now you're free to do what important people like you do.

A friend of mine told me about someone named Bob who drove him crazy. My friend was grumbling about Bob under his breath and God was listening. That night everything changed because God spoke to him as clearly as He had ever spoken to him before.

God said, "You know that person Bob who is a little slow and never quite gets things right? The one you avoid at all costs? Well, I want you to remember something. Compared to Me, you are not the sharpest knife in the drawer either, and you don't get things quite right most of the time. So next time Bob starts to bug you, remember you're My Bob."

On Their List

Have you ever listened to church people talk? You might hear things like, "Good Christians don't wear make-up," usually said by those who need to wear it. "Good Christians wouldn't have a cigar after dinner," usually said by someone who eats a half gallon of ice cream for dessert. "Good Christians don't dance," except maybe on roller skates. We all have a list, and some of you are laughing because I haven't gotten to your list.

If we're not careful, we can become narrow and self-righteous and become Super Saints. We become more religious than God. Instead of four spiritual laws, we have ten or maybe twenty. We've even developed our own vocabulary. We ask people, "When you answer the phone do you say, 'Praise the Lord?' Do you say 'Halleluiah'?" "No, I say, 'Same to ya.'" They look down at those who simply say "hello." Someone bragged to me about getting rid of his TV. "Satan's idiot box" he called it. He asked me if I had one. I was intimidated and said, "No." And I don't have one. I have two, but I didn't tell him that because I don't want to be on his list.

A pastor friend of mine is on someone's list. He bought the wrong kind of car. The first year at his church an auto dealer offered him a really good deal on a used Lincoln. It was only a year old, and it was a great deal so he bought the car. He got into real trouble because a pastor shouldn't drive a Lincoln. That was on the no-no list. He took the car back, and one of his leaders advised him to buy a new Buick. That was okay with the church people even though the new Buick cost more than the old Lincoln, but the Buick wasn't on their list. There is something spiritual about a new Buick, and something about an old Lincoln that isn't.

A pastor visited a place in the east. It was a community that didn't believe in driving cars or using electricity of any kind. They sat in their living rooms living a rigid, narrow life around kerosene lanterns. But ironically, their income came from the tobacco industry.

We sanitize and spiritualize our lists. People even take the Bible and tell me things like "I have the gift of prophecy. That means I point out everyone's mistakes and problems." I tell them, "You don't have the gift of prophecy; you have the gift of being a pain in the neck. Prophecy means to speak forth the good news." I've also noticed their family relationships aren't very healthy. When Mr. or Mrs. Right's first name is Always they are hard to live with. Maybe that's why they spend so much time at church doing a lot of prophesying and being religious.

A couple was thinking about buying a ranch. They went to meet the owner. The couple asked, "What did you name your ranch?" "Well," the owner said, "I wanted to call it the Flying W, my wife wanted to call it the Suzy-Q, one of our sons wanted to call it the Bar-J, and the other preferred the Lazy-Y, so we compromised. We called it the Flying-W Suzy-Q Bar-J Lazy-Y Ranch." "Where are all the cows?" "They couldn't survive the branding."

Have you ever been to churches where you think you can't survive the branding? There are so many lists and so much stuff and you have to do this and you can't do that. Our lists usually catch up with us.

One town in Connecticut had fifty-three residents who signed a petition to stop speeders in their town. Their patrolmen started issuing tickets, and in one morning five people were stopped. **All five had signed the petition.**

We can't even keep up with our own lists. Yet, if we're not careful, we can get to a point where we lose our joy in living because we're fixated on our list, and we're trying to force everyone to abide by it.

These people with lists have always been among us. Dr. Barnhouse, a theologian of yesteryear, was preaching at a Bible conference. Two women cornered him complaining about some young girls at the conference who weren't wearing stockings. They told Dr. Barnhouse that women at a church service should wear stockings, and they wanted him to do something about it. Keep in mind that this stocking incident happened in the 1920s. Barnhouse looked at them and said, "The Virgin Mary never wore stockings." They gasped and said, "She didn't?" He answered, "In Mary's time stockings were unknown. They were first worn by prostitutes in Italy." I love it when another pastor says stuff like that. I know he's on their list instead of me.

There are lots of lists out there. A woman confronted one pastor after the service because she had heard through the grapevine that he occasionally had a cigar. She said, "I'm praying for you, pastor." He said, "Sister, I'm praying for you, too." She said, "You don't seem to understand. I'm praying that God will help you stop that nasty habit you have." He said, "Well, Sister, you don't seem to understand either. I'm praying God will help you keep your nose out of my business."

Do you have a list? Are you checking it twice? Are you trying to figure out who is naughty or nice? Forget it. You're not Santa Claus, and you're definitely not God. At one time you were on God's list but He tore it up. Tear up your list instead of tearing up other people, and keep your nose out of God's business.

Still on the Phone

Newsweek Magazine says 91% of women and 85% of men pray. Of course 100% of golfers pray on the putting green.

What is prayer? One little girl said prayers are messages sent up at night and on Sunday when the rates are low. Often, our prayers revolve around asking God to bail us out of some mess. We're like the little girl that prayed, "God, either make Boston the capital of Vermont or lose my test paper."

Prayer can also be confusing. One little boy was saying his prayers before bed, "...Now I lay me down to sleep, I pray the Lord my soul to keep. If... If... If... If he hollers let him go, eenie, meenie, miny, mo."

Usually, we make prayers too formal, especially at church. Why do pastors pray with a "holy tone" and talk using a stained-glass voice? I like to hear new people pray at church because they haven't learned the ritual. They say things like, "Hi, God, this is Bob. Got your ears on?" That's the way prayer should be – simple. You don't have to systematize, organize, sanitize, or agonize over your prayers. Prayer is like a child coming to his father to talk.

What if I came home one day and my kids said, "Hail, thou illustrious and elegant psychologist. We welcome thee home from thy sojourn down Academy Boulevard. Wouldst thou grant to thy second daughter Kasey and thy third daughter Breanne some money that we may sojourn to yonder apothecary and procure for ourselves some cosmetics to adorn ourselves, O Gracious Father?" They don't talk like that. They would say something like, "Hi, Dad. Love you, missed you. Need to get some stuff. Got any money? Thanks, Dad."

And prayer is not just trying to persuade God to do what you want. An English professor was trying to teach his students the value of a rich vocabulary. He said to them, "If you will take a new word and use it ten times, it will be yours forever." A young woman in the class looked dreamily out the window and started saying, "George, George, George, George...." That's the way some people pray, looking for the right password to get the "George" of their dreams. Prayer is telling God you want to be a partner in what He wants to do. You won't find a better partner.

Sometimes God says "no" because you don't need what you want. Sometimes He says "no" because you have the wrong motive. Sometimes the timing is wrong, and He doesn't say "no" but rather "slow down." Other times you just aren't ready, and He doesn't say "no" or "slow" but "grow." Then there are the times when He says "go," and you can go with full confidence, knowing that it isn't just a good idea but a God idea.

A man climbed mountains as a hobby. He was climbing one of the highest mountains in the world with two professionals. They climbed up the sheltered side of the mountain to the top. As they reached the peak the man was so exhilarated he began to jump up and down to see the view. The wind was so powerful it almost blew him off the mountain. The guide quickly grabbed him and brought him down to safety and said, "On your knees, sir, on your knees. You're safe up here only on your knees."

What a statement! If you are going to get anywhere in life, especially close to the top, you're safe only on your knees. Prayer does change things. Most of the time it changes us. That is usually why God wants to spend time with us.

One little girl heard the choir singing "God Is Still on the Throne." On the way home from church she told her mom, "I really like that song 'God Is Still on the Phone.'" God *is* still on the phone. Why don't you give him a call – local, direct, and free of charge?

Be Natural

After career day in kindergarten a little girl came home all excited and told her mother that she wanted to be a nurse. Her mom said, "You don't have to be a nurse. This is America. You can be anything you want to be. You can be a doctor, an orthopedic surgeon, even the director of the whole hospital." She was excited. "I can be anything, anything at all?" As she thought about it, her eyes lit up and she exclaimed, "I want to be a horse!"

But in truth, you can't be anything you want to be. You can be only what God has designed you to be. God has designed everyone with a purpose. He put a unique seed inside of you. Just like a cantaloupe seed is designed to be a cantaloupe. Now that cantaloupe seed may decide it wants to be a watermelon. Watermelons are bigger and prettier, and they go to all of the picnics. The cantaloupe can even map out a watermelon strategy. It can buy some possibility tapes and play them over and over, "It's a possibility; I can be a watermelon," or even buy some positive thinking tapes; "You positively can be a watermelon." The cantaloupe may even obtain some subliminal tapes to play while it sleeps. The cantaloupe could even go New Age and channel up some 400-year old guru to tell it that in its other life it was a watermelon. Get a crystal and sit cross-legged and contemplate its navel while humming and think positive watermelon thoughts. Get in touch with the inner-child; perhaps its inner-child *was* a watermelon. Walk on fire and prove it's not afraid to be a watermelon. All of that can be done but when it grows, it will be a cantaloupe. It will be an insecure, dysfunctional, neurotic one, but it will be a cantaloupe because that's what God designed it to be. That was its purpose.

The only thing you are qualified to be is yourself. You can't do it all, and you can't get it all (if you did, where would you put it?). The key to life is finding your purpose, what you are created to excel in. Have you ever seen an Olympic gymnastic champion take the gold medal and also take the gold medal in the shot put; or the mechanic at the auto shop who also moonlights as an oral surgeon? It doesn't happen. Everyone has a race he is created to run. Some run the 220, others excel in the marathon, while others do better in the sprints.

Purpose is the engine of life. Without purpose we'll become like the funny cars at the circus. They are the cars with the axle off-center that just go around in circles. Clowns get on the funny cars, bounce along, go in circles, and hold on for dear life. There may be a lot of activity but there's no accomplishment. That may be funny at the circus, but it's no way to live your life. Most of us plan our vacations better than we plan our lives.

Maybe it's time for us to determine what it is we were created to do. A history teacher regularly told his class, "You can take this class one of two ways. You can take it seriously or take it over." We better take life seriously because we don't get to take it over.

Musically speaking, the bottom line is B sharp, never B flat, and always B natural. Discover what God created you to do and be. The question for us is, are we "running the race" that God designed us to run, or are we just running?

Words and Dirt, but Not Dirty Words

One man said he and his wife had words, but he never got a chance to use his. Words are powerful; they can give life or bring death. Have you ever stolen someone's joy with words or killed someone's self-esteem with words?

Motivating people is like mining for gold. When you're mining, you know you have to go through tons of dirt, but you don't go in looking for the dirt. You go in looking for the gold.

Man has been described as an earthen vessel that contains a treasure. We have a choice. We can look for the dirt (and for sure, it's there) but it will only bring hurt; or we can look for the treasure. By the way, it's easy to make a mountain out of a molehill; just add a little dirt.

Granted, we all tend to concentrate on the negative – the dirt. Think of it this way: You're having dinner at a wonderful restaurant, the atmosphere is great, the food is wonderful, and you're having a great evening. Then you start your dessert, and there's a dead fly in your chocolate mousse. Every time you think of that restaurant, you don't think of the 90% of the meal that was wonderful; you think of that bug. You never go back, although having a bug in a dessert probably happens only once every sixty years. You could eat in confidence for fifty-nine more years at a great restaurant, but you don't because you focus on the negative. Let's face it – ten years later it still bugs you.

It's natural to look for the dirt, and it starts early. I took my daughter to a huge parking lot to teach her how to ride a bike. I was excited! I said, "Breanne, I had to learn how to ride a bike on sand and rocks, but you get to ride on all this asphalt. You will go fast. You will feel the wind against your face. It's going to be wonderful! Look at all that asphalt!"

She said, "Daddy, what's that way down there?" I said, "Don't worry about that; you're going to be a bike rider. Look at all this asphalt! It's going to be great!" She said, "That's a big pole way down there." I said, "Don't worry. Look at all the asphalt! You're going to go fast!" She said, "If I run into that pole, I'll get hurt." I said, "Don't worry about hitting the pole; just look at all this asphalt."

So I put her on the bike and I grabbed the seat and ran like crazy. We were going great! Just before I let go she said, "Daddy, what if I hit the pole?" I said, "Breanne, you won't hit the pole. Look at all that asphalt." And I let her go. Breanne headed straight for the pole. She hollered, "Daddy, I'm heading for the pole." I said, "Don't worry. Look at all that asphalt on the right. Just turn right." She said, "Daddy, I can't turn right. I'm headed for the pole." I said, "Look at all the asphalt on the left.

Turn left." She said, "I can't turn left. I'm headed for the pole." She finally hit the pole, fell down, and skinned her knee. When I got there she said, "I told you I was going to hit the pole." Why did she hit the pole? Because she focused on the pole.

Most of our negative words come from our focus. Most of us are pole hitters instead of asphalt lookers. We concentrate on the negative in the parking lot of opportunity and speak negative words, which most of the time leads to a wreck on our bicycle of life. Powerful words that motivate come from the perspective of looking for the positive. Remember, forget the dirt because you'll only bring hurt, and concentrate on the treasure to motivate beyond measure. By the way, if you discover that the earthen vessels around you contain a lot of dirt, don't forget the treasure buried the deepest is usually the most valuable. So be patient and keep digging for the treasure.

Hints for the Ski Season

I'll never forget my first ski trip. I was excited: the thrill of the hill, the need for speed, man against the mountain. I was ready. I'm athletic, I'm coordinated, and I'm a macho man. If you are a first-time skier and you are feeling a little macho, allow me to give you some helpful hints as you attempt to conquer the mountains of God.

First, get the right equipment.

1.   Ski outfits cost about the same as a compact car. To save money, you can rent all this stuff by paying car rental prices, but you must sign a small legal document that clearly states this activity could possibly kill you and they are not responsible.

2.   Dressing takes at least one hour to put everything on (the ski boots are created under license from the Marquis de Sade) and two hours to get off (because you're really tired).

3.   The outfit must have four layers to make you feel like a giant radioactive spaceman.

4.   Go to the bathroom before you start putting on your equipment because if you go more than once during the day, you will have no time for skiing, and you'll think you came to the mountains to use the world's most expensive pay toilet.

Second, take ski lessons.

1.   DO NOT skip this step. Any sport with an ambulance parked at the bottom of the hill is to be respected.

2.   The skis do not come with air bags. Without a lesson, you have the life expectancy of a fruit fly. With a good lesson, you have the hope of living as long as, say, a gold fish.

3.   Tall, good-looking, blond, Swedish instructors live only in Sweden. I got a short, plump, Brooklyn girl. The first thing she showed us was how to get up. If only I had listened to her. I thought she was kidding. She told us to roll onto our stomachs, point our skis outward, and then push up with our arms. I thought she was a sadist.

4.   Learn how to stop. Use the end of your skies, not the end of your body.

5.   The chair lift does not stop. At this point I started to realize that skiing may be a little harder than I had thought. The chair lift is like a ride at Disney World. You have to jump on, then dangle in the air, and about the time you relax your realize that it doesn't stop to let you off. You have two choices: you can jump off and fall, or jump off and get hit in the back of the head by the chair (this is where the expression "between the devil and the deep blue sea" originated). I jumped and fell and then pretended to look for my contact to preserve my dignity.

Third, learn the laws of skiing gravity.

1.   Your instructor has a hidden anti-gravity drive. She doesn't fall.

2.   Little kids whiz by too dumb to know about gravity. Makes you want to trip them.

3.   You will spend most of the day trying to defy the force that pulls you downward – your skis down the hill and your body (fanny and face mostly) down in the snow.

I survived the day by staying on the Peter Rabbit Hill. I was mad at my equipment. My toes hurt. I questioned God and why he made mountains. I told myself I would never ski again. I quit! The next day I was sore. Penny said, "I can't believe you're sore. You jog two miles every day." I told her I hardly ever fall down or hit trees when I jog. She said, "Practice what you teach. 'If you can take it, you can make it.'" I hate it when someone quotes me.

I'm still not very good. Skiing remains a contact sport for me. I'm looking for skis with airbags. I warm up every year by running up a flight of stairs and coming back down without using my legs. It's a great bun warmer for the kind of hot dog skiing I do.

A few years ago some buddies talked me into going up on top of the mountain. Supposedly there was an easy way down, but when we got there the run was closed and we had to get on a "black run," which is color coded to mean "Today you will meet God." Actually the name of the run was Pall Bearers Peak. Ski people ought to take a course in public relations. Would a cereal sell if it was named Death? No, they call it Life. It would never work to say, "Mikey, come try a spoonful of death." The ski runs should be named something like Marshmallow Satin or Easy Comfort. Anyway, I looked down this mountain. Way down! I was telling God I would be a foreign missionary when I heard the voice of a friend.

Tim said, "Charles, just follow me." So I did. Tim is an expert skier. He knew the best way down and was willing to stay with me. On the slope of life it is great to have someone to follow.

Miracles Out of Messes

I'd had my share of mess-ups even before I became a speaker. In my last year of graduate school during Psychotherapy practicum, I was given my first patient. Thinking I was the next Sigmund Freud, I grew a beard, smoked a pipe and looked psychological.

My patient had test anxiety, and I was to do relaxation training, slowly relaxing him so he could take a test. My instructors were watching through a one-way mirror.

Psychologists like to be behind one-way mirrors because every psychologist has a little of the voyeur in him. It has been said that when a pretty girl enters a room, people watch the pretty girl, but a psychologist watches the people watch the pretty girl. I was never that good – I always watched the pretty girl.

I started the relaxation training of my patient, and he went to sleep. He was supposed to relax, not sleep. How could I do the procedure? The guy began to snore, and I panicked. I looked at the one-way mirror for advice, and all I could see was myself looking stupid. I panicked some more. I figured I needed to wake him. I grabbed him by the arm and shouted, "Wake up!" a lot louder than I intended.

He woke up, panicked, and pulled away. I reached for him as he headed for the door, and then I went after him. I wasn't going to lose my first patient. He ran faster and so did I. He ran down the stairs; I followed. He went out the psychological service center, and I ran after him. Then I realized this didn't look good – chasing people out of the psychological service center. I was discouraged. I thought I'd be kicked out of the program.

I went back to the room, and the one-way mirror was shaking. I thought that was weird, so I opened the door and saw two grown psychologists falling out of their chairs, laughing so hard tears were running down their cheeks, and one was banging his head against the mirror. They said that was the funniest thing they had ever seen. Too bad we didn't videotape it so we could show it to students for generations to come as an example of how not to perform relaxation training.

I survived, became a psychologist, and then went to work at a church counseling center, but my mess-ups went with me. I'll never forget the time the pastor was sick and I had to do the baptisms. All I could think of was the pledge of allegiance. It was patriotic, but it wasn't exactly what was needed.

Nowadays people don't even notice most mess-ups at church. Most of the people don't know Joan of Arc from Noah's Ark. But there are some mess-ups no one can miss. My all time mess-up was at the historic First Baptist Church of Dallas. For almost 100 years, this was the pulpit from which Dr. Truett and Dr. Criswell had preached. When I made my mistake, Dr. Truett probably turned over in his grave, and Dr. Criswell probably wished for his.

I was speaking on "The Symptoms of Depression" and was going to say that one symptom of depression is erratic sleep patterns. But it came out "erotic sleep patterns." I even got an "amen" from a deacon. It brought the house down. After the seminar on depression, I was depressed.

I did the same series in Oklahoma and said it right. So when I concluded the series and packaged it for tape sales, we included the tape from Oklahoma that had "erratic" instead of "erotic" on the tape. No one wanted that series. They wanted the one where I messed up. So we put the original tape back in. It resulted in being the best selling series of the year, and we heard numerous stories of changed lives. People listened to the series because they wanted to hear the mess-up.

I guess that is what relaxes me most about speaking – I have a great back up. God takes my messes and makes miracles. God must be thinking, "With Charles, I'll never run out of material."

A Voice Like His

I was eating lunch with a man who was taking a pill. When I asked him why he was taking it, he said he was taking it for his colitis. I asked him who he was colliding with. Our words can collide with people and condemn them, or our words can confirm them. The Bible says that pleasant words are like a honeycomb. In that day, honey was a remedy for sicknesses such as a sore throat. It was also an energy booster.

Our words are an overflow of our hearts. What is on the inside will come out in our words. Two brothers were getting on in years, and one was envious of the other. The older of the two asked God, 'Why has my brother been blessed with wealth and happiness and I have nothing? All my life I've never missed a single day without saying my morning and evening prayers. My church attendance has been perfect. I've not made a single decision without first calling Your name. And now as I'm nearing my final days I'm in church every day and almost every night. Yet, I can hardly afford to pay my meager rent. My brother, on the other hand, drinks and gambles. Not once have I seen him in church, yet my brother has more money than he can count. So I ask you, God, not to punish my brother, but to tell me why you've allowed him such wealth and happiness and I've been left with nothing?" God replied, "Because you are such a self-righteous pain in the neck."

Why do we use condemning words? Because we are self-righteous pains in the neck. The use of words is mentioned a lot more in the Bible than gambling and drinking. Yet we are so self-righteous. "You don't see me down at the casino. You don't see me doing this or that." What about your words? The Book says that our lives and our lips are connected.

Perhaps we use condemning words because we think this will make others change their behavior. Our motives are good but our methods aren't. I'll share a personal experience. I speak at quite a few banquets (which, by the way, I need more of in December). Many times the food is incredible, with great desserts. This year I had two banquets on successive nights in different cities. At the first banquet, the dessert was a wonderful cheesecake with a caramel nut topping. As we sat down to eat, the pastor told me that he thought I looked as if I had put on a few pounds. He said that it looked like being on the road was making me a "big" psychologist. Now you would have thought that those words would have kept me from eating the cheesecake. Actually, the opposite happened. I ate the whole thing. I needed comfort. I was feeling a little let down; my self-esteem was suffering. Remember, it is what is eating you – not what you are eating, that makes a difference.

What made this incident stand out in my mind was that the next night's banquet had the same cheesecake. I had already decided to eat it. My friend Jack Graham happened to be sitting at my table. One of the first things he said to me was that he thought I had lost weight and that I really looked good. He said that he was proud of me because he knew how difficult it is to be on the road and keep the weight off. I didn't eat the cheesecake. Why? Because Jack's words boosted my confidence so much that I didn't need the comfort food. I discovered that good words are like honey; they fill you up but without the calories.

A pastor who was recovering from surgery was going to miss seeing his son Chris run in the state cross-country championship meet. He asked his brother, Merv, to go in his place. He told his brother, "I can't be there to see Chris run so I want you there. At the beginning of the race, holler a lot; then at the end, I want you to really cheer loudly, and I want you to make your voice sound like mine." Merv heeded the advice, and Chris ran a strong race, finishing second. Merv, also a pastor, discerned the theological truth in the story. "That's what God wants us to do," he said. "Make your voice sound like mine."

God says, "Charles, I've got some people in the family who are in the race, too. I want you to be there and say words of encouragement. I want your voice to sound like Mine." God is our advocate. He's on our team, and he's cheering for us.

After attending a Christmas concert, a journalism student wrote down this beautiful Christmas reflection:

When I settled into a chair near the back of the auditorium, the old gentleman next to me began telling me that his son was a tenor in the choir. "He's very good," the man said. "I'm sure you'll enjoy his singing."

The curtain rose, revealing a choir of one hundred young men and women. They began to sing, and it wasn't long before the old man was nudging me and pointing out his son, "He sings beautifully, doesn't he?" he asked. Although I strained to hear the boy, it was impossible to single him out. Yet I'm certain that his father could. Our Father is the same with us. Though we are all part of the mighty chorus of believers, He hears us one at a time. I want my voice to sound like His.

6

Attitude

If attitude is the crayon that colors life and your favorite color is black, then you need this chapter. If you would like to be a promoter instead of a provoker, a contributor instead of a complainer, a bandage instead of a bruise, a blesser instead of a blaster, read on.

Falling Isn't That Bad

Many people believe the basic fears are fear of falling, fear of abandonment, and fear of loud noises. If, when you were a kid, your mother abandoned you by throwing you out of a three-story window and you made a loud noise when you hit the ground, I don't think I can help you, but the rest of you, read on.

A certain amount of fear is a good thing. It's normal. Normal fear directs us to look both ways before crossing the street. Abnormal fear prevents us from crossing the street. Denying our fears will cause us to cross the street without looking either way.

Facing fear is difficult but necessary. Face your fears by admitting that you are afraid. Kids are more open about their fears than adults. One kid was really afraid of a big storm. His mother came in to comfort him. He said, "Mommy, will you stay in my room tonight?" She said, "No, I have to stay with Daddy." As she turned to go, she heard him say under his breath, "Daddy! That big sissy."

A little girl who was afraid of the dark went into her parents' room and told her mother she was scared. Her mother said, "It's okay, sweetheart, there's nothing to be afraid of, God is in there with you." The little girl went back to her bed and as she climbed in she said, "God, if you are in here, don't you say a word or you'll scare me to death." Kids are open with their fears.

Why should we face our fear? Living with fear has consequences. You've heard the expressions "scared stiff" or "scared to death." Fear makes you *frail*. At a symposium a physician spoke on psychosomatic medicine. The doctor said, "In spite of what they say, almost all chronic patients who see a physician have one problem. That problem did not start with a cough, chest pain, or hyperacidity. In most cases the first symptom was fear." Fear makes you sick.

Not only that, fear makes you *fumble*. When you're afraid, you have a tendency not to do well. The pressure is so great that it causes you to mess up.

It's like the guy who was out of money. He decided to rob the bank because he couldn't think of any other way to get money. He didn't know anything about robbing banks, so he practiced what he would say over and over. He got the sack to put the money in and a revolver, and then practiced sticking the sack over a counter and pointing the gun in someone's face saying, "Don't mess with me. This is a stick up." When it came time for the real thing, he was really nervous but also confident that he had it down pat. However, when he got into the bank, fear took over and he handed the lady the revolver, raised the sack, and said, "Don't stick with me. This is a mess up."

Fear can also make you *frantic*, causing you to be paralyzed to inaction or instead, causing you to make a terrible mistake.

Remember the children's story "Chicken Little"? Chicken Little thought the sky was falling. She told Henny Penny the sky was falling, and the animals stampeded. At last, they met Mr. Fox who offered them refuge in his den. Because of their panic, they accepted, and Mr. Fox had a feast.

Fear can also make you look *foolish*. A friend of mine was a starter on the football team his sophomore year. He fielded the opening kick-off, broke through the defensive line, and started running down the sidelines. As he was running, he glanced to his right and saw the shadow of somebody chasing him. He ran faster, but the guy stayed right behind him. To avoid being tackled, when he got close to the goal line he *dove* into the end-zone. He looked back and there was no one behind him. The stadium lights were such that it was his own shadow he was running from. People end up running from their own shadows and doing foolish things. If you don't face your fears, fears will bully you into a life of protection instead of progression.

Have you ever had to deal with a bully? When I was in second grade, I had a bully in my life who would knock me down, push my books off the desk, and call me names. I was so miserable. Finally I got sick of it and decided to face the bully. I turned to her and said, "Look, I'm tired of this." You know what? She stopped.

Abnormal fear will make you frail, fumbling, and frantic. It will make you do foolish things and eventually cause you to fail.

One time when I was taking a snow skiing lesson the ski instructor came by and knocked me down. I asked him why he did that and he said, "I noticed that you have made a lot of progress until today. Today, you're making no progress because you are trying to keep from falling. You're not enjoying this, and you're tense. I just wanted to show you that falling isn't that bad."

Are you really enjoying life, or are you just trying not to fall?

Nifty at Fifty

It finally happened. I got my invitation to join the retirement association, AARP, the American Association of the Really Pooped or something like that. They were a little early. I guess they were preparing me. This summer I will be fifty years old. It's the autumn of life, and everything seems to be heading south. I guess it really hit me when I filled out a survey and checked the box marked 45-55 and realized I was in the next to the last box.

I can't wait to get all the cards that say things like, "It's your fiftieth birthday. Ahead of you is adventure, romance, challenge, and a lot of other good reading, too."

I admit things seem to be changing. My hair is starting to wrinkle on the way up and now comes out of my ears instead of the top of my head. There appears to be more sand in the bottom of the hourglass. My narrow waist and broad mind have started to trade places. I notice that there is usually a noisy crash when I park the car. That funny face that I used to make in the mirror when I was a kid – well, the mirror is now getting even.

My diet has changed. I can remember when bacon and eggs and sunshine were good for you. Now I eat cream of wheat, wheat crackers, wheat germ, and wheat shrimp. I long for a cholesterol picnic of fried chicken. Somehow the enzyme that digests everything is gone.

I guess the psychological changes are what bother me most. I can still do a lot of things physically. I can still merge in traffic and drive at night, but I admit the gleam in my eye is usually the reflection from my bifocals.

Most of the time I'd prefer a hot bath to a hot date. I think part of the problem is the bath water. I never had a bath in my adult life until this year. I always took showers. Then I took a bath, and all of a sudden I'm fifty. If you're doing great with showers, don't take baths.

What really concerns me is that I'm acting like I'm old. I drive around town with others and tell them what's no longer there. I holler out gas prices. My dad used to do that, and I didn't understand why. At a certain age you can't go by a gas station without hollering out the gas prices. Maybe a Gas Price Support Group would help.

I get the feeling I'm on Golden Pond and my boat is sinking. I'm not going to let it get to me, though. I can still walk down memory lane without getting lost. I'm going to enjoy the grandbabies. I love keeping them. It doesn't matter that they get up five times a night – so do I. As a matter of fact, I told my wife since we get up five times a night anyway to go to the bathroom, why don't we have a baby? The only problem is we would forget where we put it.

I'm not going to get depressed because most of my dreams haven't come true. However, one did. I can remember when my mother combed my hair when I was a kid and I dreamed that I didn't have any.

I admit my body has changed. My back goes out more than I do. But I'm not old. I'm chronologically gifted. I have experience. I may be a little over the hill, but I'm not under it. I'm going to enjoy life. I'm learning ways to look young. I sit in public and eat prunes. Since they are so wrinkled, I look great.

Getting older has benefits. People let me cut in line at the checkout counter. They think I'm having difficulty breathing. I've just had to learn to do some things to adjust. I need to clear my throat occasionally so the cleaning lady doesn't dust me. There are a lot of other great things about growing older. I wish I could remember some of them. I do remember my body is wrinkled but my soul is fresh. I'm not going to give up. I'm going to look up. I'm not going to retire. I'm going to refire.

So when you see the glow in the sky coming from the west, it's my birthday cake. People will stand around it to keep warm because heat is good for their arthritis. I want you to know that I will amaze my friends and blow out all of the candles, even if that sets off the smoke alarm. It's going to be nifty to be fifty. Although my reflexes may be slow, I still have a lot of get up and go. Like all great runners, as I finish the race, I'm picking up the pace.

Snapshot of Encouragement

How many of you get too much encouragement? Do people tell you how wonderful you are everywhere you go? When you get to work does everyone stop and clap for you? When you arrive home do you get a standing ovation? Do your kids carry pictures of you in their wallets and show them to everyone saying, "These are my parents. Aren't they wonderful?" As a matter of fact, all of us need encouragement. A good rule to remember is that if people are breathing, they need some encouragement.

Most of us probably feel like the traveling salesman who once walked into a restaurant and said to the waitress, "Bring me some burnt toast, watered-down scrambled eggs, and some weak cold coffee." The waitress said with some doubt, "Yeah, sure. What else would you like?" "Just sit across from me," the man pleaded, "and nag me. I'm terribly homesick." Unfortunately sometimes we're not homesick but heresick. A little boy was at summer camp, and one of the counselors saw him sitting on his cot looking very despondent. He said, "What's the matter Billy? Are you homesick?" Billy answered, "No, I'm heresick." Homesick or heresick – the cure is encouragement.

On some days life throws you a fastball, and you don't even have on a glove. But no matter how well or how poorly you're doing, no one suffers from too much encouragement. People need encouragement when they least deserve it.

In the play *A Raisin in the Sun*, there's a scene where Walter has lost all of the family's savings that were intended to make their dream come true. Now their dream has dried up like "a raisin in the sun." Beneatha is so disgusted with her brother that she says, "There ain't nuthin' left to love." In a climactic, emotion-filled moment, Mama puts her hands on her daughter's shoulders, looks her directly in the eyes, and says: "Child, when do you think is the time to love somebody the most;

when they done good and made things easy for everybody? Well, then, you ain't through learning – because that ain't the time at all. It's when he's at his lowest and can't believe in hisself 'cause the world done whipped him so."

Not giving up on people keeps them from giving up. Jackie Robinson rose through the ranks of the Afro-American Baseball league to become the first black pro-baseball player. The first year in the major leagues was a horrible year for him. All across the country, people yelled racial slurs and insults at him. He said the turning point of his life was in Cincinnati, the hometown of Peewee Reese, the famous Dodgers' shortstop. The fans were hurling insults at Jackie Robinson and calling him names when, during a delay of the game, Peewee Reese walked over and put his arm around Jackie Robinson and just stood there for a moment for the entire world to see. Peewee Reese was saying, "He's my teammate. He's in my family. He's part of me." From then on Jackie Robinson said that he knew he would be able to make it.

One of the more obscure exhibits in the Smithsonian Institution is a display of the personal effects found on Abraham Lincoln the night he was shot. They include a small handkerchief embroidered A. Lincoln, a country boy's pen knife, a spectacle case repaired with cotton string, a Confederate five-dollar bill, and a worn-out newspaper clipping extolling his accomplishments as President. It begins, "Abe Lincoln is one of the greatest statesmen of all time...." Why would our nation's sixteenth President carry around a clipping like that? History remembers Lincoln as a folk hero and a President's President. Was Lincoln an egomaniac? Hardly. When Lincoln was President, he wasn't as popular as he became after his death. The nation was bitterly divided, and Lincoln's leadership was constantly threatened. He was the object of a critical press. So Abraham Lincoln needed something in his pocket to remind him that his critics were not his only observers. He carried an icon of affirmation, something that reminded him that someone believed in him.

Encourage people by telling them how much you believe in them. Find someone who is breathing and offer a word of encouragement. She might not carry a picture of you in her wallet, but I suspect she will carry a snapshot of you in her heart.

Ups and Downs of Life

Sometimes I get down – so low that I could play racquetball on the curb. It helps to understand why you're down. It might even help change DOWN to UP. Let me explain.

These things can bring you **D.O.W.N:**

DUMB ACTS - Wearing your baseball hat backwards to a job interview unless you want to be an umpire, and standing between a dog and a fire hydrant are dumb acts. A tourist driving down a country road came to this sign: "Road Closed – Do Not Enter." The road ahead looked good, and being an experienced traveler, he ignored the sign and pressed on. Five miles later he came to a washed-out bridge and had to retrace his route. When he reached the same warning sign, on the back it said: "Welcome Back, Stupid!"

OTHER PEOPLE - People are irritating. I had a secretary who wouldn't answer the phone. I asked why and she responded, "Why should I? Nine out of ten times it's for you."

Other people can also be grumpy. The seven dwarfs had a great life. They worked in a diamond mine and whistled while they worked, yet one of them was Grumpy. Nearly every crowd has a Grumpy.

WORLD – The world is often a difficult place to live: the mate that snores is the one who falls asleep first, and the line you're in is the longest and the slowest.

NEW THINGS in your life can also bring you down. Change is difficult. The standard typewriter keyboard is an example. The most frequently used keys are located as far apart as possible to slow down your typing speed. Keys on the machines of the 1800s jammed if the typist were too fast. About forty years ago, a keyboard called the Dvorak Simplified Keyboard was developed with most frequently used keys in the home row. The right hand does more work (56%) than the left, and tests show that typists greatly increase their speed (up to five times) with no increase in errors. Still, we labor with a keyboard designed to be inefficient. Why? Change is difficult.

Lucy told Charlie Brown, "I'd like to change the whole world, Charlie Brown." And Charlie Brown said, "Where would you start, Lucy?" She said, "I'd start with you."

Yes, lots of things can bring us down, but we don't have to stay down. Let's look at the same word (down) from an UP perspective.

Dumb things we do can make us smarter. A coach once said, "The reason one play succeeds is that the play before it failed." Failure can make us wiser. Every good skier was once a bad skier. Every good speaker was once a bad speaker. Every golfer...well... is still a bad golfer. The principle still works.

Others can irritate you but the irritations are necessary. Disorganized people hate organized people. I have piles and they have files. But guess what? When I can't find it in my piles, I need someone with files to insure I have what I need. We need others in order to be successful. Your weaknesses are often others' strengths. Others can build you up.

World – The world that weighs you down can make you stronger. Difficulties develop you. Lifting weights strengthens you. The weights suddenly feel lighter, but they haven't changed; your muscles have become stronger.

New Things are good things. Years ago, a bishop on the East Coast paid his annual visit to a small religious college. Engaging in after-dinner conversation with the college president, he said that the millennium could not be long in coming since everything in nature had been discovered and all inventions had been made. The president disagreed saying that human beings would be flying through the skies like the birds within a relatively short time. "Nonsense!" shouted the bishop. "Flight is reserved for the angels!" The bishop's name was Wright. He had two sons: Orville and Wilbur.

New things – ideas, ways, people, and situations – may cause stress but on the positive side. They can get us out of our comfort zone. New Things are the basis of life. UP means that Ultimately there is a Purpose.

A tribe of Indians lived next to a swift and dangerous river that swept away any who fell in. They were attacked by a hostile group, and their only way of escape was to cross the river. They placed their children, wounded, and elderly on their backs and trudged into the river. To their surprise, the extra weight steadied their footing and they safely reached the other side.

Circumstances that you believe are keeping you DOWN may be what allow you to climb UP. Your burden may actually be your blessing. Your down could really be up!

Take Dead Aim

I like New Years Day. It's a New Year, and I'm glad. As a matter of fact, I stayed up New Year's Eve just to make sure the old year left and to address a few Christmas cards. I do procrastinate a little. But there is also a down side to a New Year. For example, your car has depreciated another $1,000, and your wife's clothes are out of style. However, there is something refreshing and energizing about a fresh start.

I guess you heard about the guy who stormed into the newspaper office and said, "I want to see the guy in charge of the obituaries." Some clerk pointed to a rookie reporter and said, "Over there." The guy stormed over and angrily said, "Young man, I want to let you know that my name appeared in your obituary column, and as you can see I am as alive as you are and I want you to do something about it. I want you to print a retraction in tomorrow's paper." The young reporter replied, "Well, sir, we don't print retractions in the obituary column, but let me tell you what I'll do. I'll put you in tomorrow's birth column, and you can have a fresh start."

The New Year is a fresh start. At my age, I need a fresh start to finally get it together before it all falls apart. It's time to make some resolutions for a better year. I discovered it's easier to make resolutions for other people. It's easier to see what they can do to have a better year than what I can do. It's great to have a time of beginning again. It's easier to get a clean sheet of paper than to erase over the one you have. The New Year is like a clean sheet of paper.

Most people don't do so well with their New Year's Resolutions. Health clubs are full in January, but they begin to thin out in February (no pun intended). People get off to great starts in things like exercise programs. It's 1..2..3 and then slower 1......2......3...... and then it's 9...1...1. The problem is that the New Year's resolutions collide with the old year's habits.

We've all picked up some bad habits. Bad habits are like a comfortable bed. They're easy to get into and hard to get out of. I know how habits can sneak up on you. Years ago I was having some stomach problems. I thought it was because I speak at a lot of banquets and end up eating a lot of rubber chicken late at night. I went to the doctor, and at first he thought I had an ulcer. I told him, "I can't have an ulcer. I'm a stress expert and that would destroy my career." It would be like a fitness expert getting stuck in the golden arches. I was getting a little stressed. Of course it wasn't an ulcer. My wife made the correct diagnosis. I had to have my gall bladder removed. She had been telling me for years that I had too much gall.

While I was talking to the doctor, he asked me about my habits. He asked me if I drank a lot of water. I told him, "No, I drink Diet Coke." He asked "How many?" I told him, "More than most people." "How many is that?" I said, "More than I should." He asked, "How many exactly?" I said, "More than the general population." The doctor said, "Charles, give me a number between two and twenty. How many do you drink a day?" I said, "Ten." He said, "That's too many." I looked at him and said, "I know. I've been trying to tell you that for the last ten minutes." He wanted me to be specific about my habit, and I wanted to keep it general. When you're specific about a habit, you bring it to a conscious level and then you have a problem. In other words you have to move to another state. You leave the state of denial and enter the state of I-need-to-do-something.

Changes are not made in general. That's why you can go to a general church and hear a general sermon about general things and you can decide in general that you are going to generally do better and what you generally do is what you generally did before you generally went in there and generally you won't do anything different, in general, generally speaking. Why? Changes have to be specific.

When you begin a New Year, new month, or new life, start by thinking about what specific changes you need to make to be what God created you to be. What is important and unique about you? Often you have to stop doing many things so that you can do the main thing. You may not be able to do what everybody wants you do to in order for you to do what God called you to do. The key to doing more may be to do less, but do it well.

A TV anchor has a plaque on his desk that says, "Is what I am doing right now benefiting the broadcast?" The plaque reminds him to do the specific things that allow him to accomplish the main thing. The late golf teacher, Harvey Pennick, says to take dead aim. In other words, don't try to hit the ball in a general direction but aim for a specific place. Today is a new day, a fresh start. Make specific plans and take dead aim.

Talking Heads

One little girl complained to her mother that she had a stomachache and didn't feel like going to church. Her mother said, "Your stomach hurts because it's empty. It will feel better when you put something in it." They went to church, and, as they were leaving, the pastor mentioned that he had a headache. The little girl told him, "Your head hurts because it's empty. It will feel better when you put something in it."

In a way, she was right because how you feel is basically determined by what you put in your head. Thoughts are the seeds you're planting for future attitudes. What you think today is what you will do tomorrow. Thinking occurs when your mouth stays shut and your head keeps talking. You are way ahead of the game if you realize that you talk to yourself. We control the mind; then the mind controls us. Input controls output.

A friend of mine was house-training his dog. Every time the dog made a mess in the house, he hit the dog with a paper and threw the dog out the window. After about three weeks, I asked how it was going. He said, "The dumb dog makes a mess and then jumps out the window." The dog learned the wrong thing, and many of us grew up also learning the wrong things.

Most stress is caused from our thinking patterns. Many think they have to always be right or always win. The problem is, to be right they have to find someone who's wrong, and to win they have to find someone who will lose.

Change your thinking. For example, rather than thinking "I have to be right," try "I need to be helpful." Next time you are in a traffic jam try thinking that this is the only twenty minutes of uninterrupted time you will have all day to pray or listen to good music. Isn't that better than working yourself into a heart attack or stroke and blowing your horn and getting angry at inanimate objects?

Stressful people think more about what they don't have than what God has provided. In 1911, the Mona Lisa was stolen from the Louvre Museum in Paris. It was missing for two years. During that time, more people came to the museum to stare at the blank space than had come to view the masterpiece itself in the previous twelve years. Doesn't that sound like us? We take for granted all the masterpieces in our lives until they become blank spaces. Think about your gains instead of your losses. Think about the donut and not the hole.

How you think about God determines whether you respond or react to the world. If you're sick and *react* to the medication, that's not good. But if you *respond* to the medication, that is good. That's the way it is in the world. I want to respond and not just react to my environment.

With the starting quarterback injured and the second string quarterback not even dressed because of illness, only the freshman quarterback, with no college game experience other than punting, was all the coach had left. It was first down with the ball resting on their own three-yard line. The coach's main thought was just to get away from the goal line so the team would have room to punt out of danger. The coach said, "Son, I want you to hand-off to Jones, our big fullback, for the next two plays. Let him run into the middle of the line and get us a few yards. Then I want you to punt." The young quarterback did as he was instructed. On the first play he handed off to Jones, but miraculously Jones found a hole off tackle and ran fifty yards. The young quarterback called the same play again and once more, miracle of miracles, the hole was there again. This time Jones ran forty-five yards. The fans were going crazy. The ball was on the opponent's two-yard line, only six short feet from the goal line. Confidently the team lined up quickly and the young quarterback received the snap, stepped back and punted the football into the stands. As the team came off the field, the coach angrily grabbed the young quarterback and asked, "What in the world were you thinking when you called that last play?" The quarterback answered blankly, "I was thinking what a dumb coach we have."

Your thoughts about your "life coach" will often determine your stress level. If you think your coach has a good plan for your life, you can relax as you run the plays you've been given. God says the plans he has for us are good. If your life is aching, maybe you ought to consider the little girl's advice. For a life ache I bet she would say, "Your life hurts because it is empty. Put something in it and you'll feel better." Put some good thoughts in your head, and you'll discover that when you change your thinker, life isn't such a stinker.

Something to Think About

Our thinking often influences how we feel. If it rains on Saturday, the farmers are happy and the golfers are sad. It's the same rain, but they're thinking different thoughts about the rain.

I first learned the importance of how we think when I was at the mental health clinic (remember, I was on staff, not actually in the mental health clinic). We had diagnostic meetings every afternoon – boring meetings. I thought, "How could I liven up these meetings?" One day I found a gorilla suit. Now, why was a gorilla suit at the mental health clinic? I don't know. It looked as if some monkey business was going on, but I decided I could use this to liven up the meeting that day. So... when everyone was in the room, I charged into the meeting in the gorilla suit. Everyone took off running. (You see, you never totally relax when you work at a mental health clinic.) I chased a nurse down the hall. Finally, she reached the end of the hall with no place to go. She turned around and looked pretty bad – somewhere between migraine headache and acid indigestion. I thought I had done enough damage so I took off the gorilla head and said, "It's not a gorilla. It's not a patient. It's me, Dr. Lowery." I won't tell you what she said; it wasn't very nice. What she thought had stressed her out and, of course, she blamed it on me.

How many of us are letting our thoughts stress us out? You see, in one way the body is incredibly dumb. It just does what the brain tells it to do. It doesn't have to be true. It just has to think it's true. For example, when I get a headache, I tell Penny I'm going to take an Advil. Later, when she asks how my headache is, I tell her, "It's a lot better. That Advil sure works." She says, "That's amazing because, though you got the pills out, you left them on the counter." You see, I don't have to take an Advil for my headache; I just have to *think* I've taken an Advil for my headache.

Let me illustrate how thinking can mean the difference between work and play. A man came home from work every day, sat in his recliner, and enjoyed a little peace and quiet. But one day the neighborhood boys discovered that the man's backyard was a natural ball field. So they started playing ball there every afternoon, making lots of noise and disturbing our friend. He would go outside and holler at them, trying to make them leave, but they'd always come back. He finally called the local sheriff, who ran them off. But the next day they were back. Then our friend had an idea. He went outside and called the kids. Finally they came. He apologized and said he was sorry he'd run them off. He said he'd really learned to enjoy the noise they made and asked if they would come and make noise again. If they would, he would pay each of them a quarter. They were excited and showed up the next day and made lots of noise. He asked them to come back the next day and make noise and he would pay them again. He said this every day but kept lowering their pay a nickel until he was down to paying them just one nickel. And he said, "I really want you to come back tomorrow and make noise, but I can only pay you a penny. Will you come?" They said, "No, we're not playing for a penny." They got mad and never came back to play, and our man is enjoying his peace and quiet.

What happened? Our friend was able to change their thinking. At first, playing ball was fun, but when they were paid, they started thinking of it as work. And of course if you don't get paid for your work, you quit.

Thinking . . . WOW! It really is important. No wonder Yogi Berra said, "Baseball is 90% mental and the other half is physical."

Now, before you buy the next positive thinking book, let me tell you that just changing your thinking is not the total answer. When I worked for the state hospital, I met a man dressed in an ornate military outfit who said he was Napoleon and he was inquiring about the location of his armies. I made up a little rhyme about it:

He had great self-esteem
And was a positive thinker,
But his thinking was not true,
You may think that I'm a stinker,
For I told him he was at Waterloo.

Thinking has to be based on reality and truth. You may be able to convince yourself the E on your gas gauge stands for *enough*, but your car is going to be much harder to convince. You could play it a motivational tape to encourage it or you could paint it to improve its self-esteem or move it to another neighborhood thinking that all it needs is a change of scenery. But your car will only go when you give it some fuel. So fuel your faith and act on some positive thoughts. Now, that's something to think about.

So You Think You Had a Bad Day?

When you got up this morning was the bird singing outside your window a buzzard? Did you put your pants on backwards and they fit better? Did you wake up to discover that your waterbed had leaked and then realized you don't have a waterbed? You may be tempted to have a pity party and invite only yourself so that you get all the pity and all the refreshments (four or five Snickers). I want to tell you it isn't as bad as you think. Listen to what happened to Mr. Jones.

One day Mrs. Jones decided to get rid of some bad hair spray that she had. She decided that a good way to get rid of it would be to spray it into the commode. Shortly afterwards, he husband, Mr. Jones, came home. As was his usual custom, he went to the "reading room" (bathroom) to relax. As soon as he was comfortably seated, he lit a cigarette and tossed the match between his legs into the commode. YOU GUESSED IT! The hair spray exploded and blew Mr. Jones heavenward (or sideward). Unfortunately for Mr. Jones, the shower bar stopped his ascent. So, after the ambulance arrived, the driver asked Mrs. Jones how Mr. Jones got both a burned backside and a concussion at the same time. She began to explain what had happened as the ambulance attendants were carrying Mr. Jones down the stairs. The ambulance drivers got so tickled about the story that they dropped Mr. Jones down the stairs and broke both his arms. Poor Mr. Jones. It definitely was not his day. He suffered one burned backside, one concussion, and two broken arms.

Now don't you feel better already? Look for something good, something to be thankful for. I'm thankful I'm not married to Shirley MacLaine. With three daughters, shopping is a pain; but if Shirley were my wife I would have to shop for things that had a four or five lifetime guarantee because Shirley is born again and again and again. You can always find something to be thankful for.

If you can't think of anything to be thankful for, read the paper and be thankful it didn't happen to you. One guy told me he couldn't be thankful because he couldn't even pay his bills. I told him to be thankful he wasn't his creditor. One little boy said he was thankful for his glasses. "They keep girls from kissing me and boys from hitting me."

If you still can't find anything to be thankful for, be thankful for your nose. Be thankful God put it on right side up. What if God had put your nose on upside down? If it rained, you would drown, and if you sneezed, you would blow your thankless head off.

See, I "nose" you feel better already.

Rise and Whine

A man joined the military, and he was issued his identification tag. It noted his blood type (Rh factor) and his religion. Following his name and serial number were the words "A negative Protestant."

Here are some questions for you. Do you see dark clouds in every silver lining? Do you find the difficulty in every opportunity? Do you wear black just in case someone dies? If you smell flowers, do you immediately look for a coffin? Do you shake heads instead of hands? If you answered "yes," you're going to be seasick for the entire voyage of life.

There have always been two groups of people. Remember the First Church of the Promised Land relocation committee? One group came back with grapes and one group came back with gripes.

Most gripers have a pained expression on their face. Charles Spurgeon was talking to some young preachers about the importance of maintaining a proper facial expression when they preach. He said, "Now, when you preach on heaven, you ought to wear a smile; joy ought to radiate on your face." One of the young whippersnappers on the front row asked, "Well, Dr. Spurgeon, what's your face supposed to look like when you preach on hell?" He said, "Just look normal, young man, just look normal."

Where did we get the idea that the more religion you have, the more painful your face ought to look? One guy was asked if he were a minister. He said, "No, I've just been sick for a few weeks."

Sometimes it's hard to tell who the gripers are by their outside appearance. They have a religious smile until you're around them for a while. I wish we could tell them apart so when I see them coming, I could run the other way. It would be great if God would turn all the negative people positive. But if He won't do that, He could at least turn their ankles so we would know them by their limp.

The gripers are everywhere. In fact, a little bit of elder brother is in all of us – faithful, yet complaining. We are never satisfied.

I heard a great story about a grandmother taking her little grandson to the beach. She put a sun-hat on him, and he brought his little bucket and shovel. After they were settled, Grandma went to sleep. All of a sudden she woke up and realized the boy was gone. "What's happened?" she thought. She looked out and saw the boy had drifted far out into the ocean. People were in a panic, screaming and hollering. She got on her knees and prayed desperately for God to save him. Just then a huge wave came roaring in and the little boy was dumped right in front of her. She looked at the boy, then looked up toward heaven, put her hands on her hips, and said, "Lord, he had a hat on when I lost him."

The gripers just look for a reason to be mad – like the guy who hadn't kissed his wife in thirty years and then shot the first man who did. You ask negative people how they feel and their answer sounds like an episode out of *General Hospital*. If people try to help, they just look disgusted. They don't want a solution; they want to be miserable. Heaven has no sickness, no pain, and no problems, so people who enjoy being miserable won't like it. I guess God will have to put in a suggestion box, or it won't be heaven for these people. They're against everything. If they drowned, you'd have to look for them upstream. They have the faces of joyless toads and live life with their lower lips stuck out. Some have been in a bad mood for forty years. If the joy of Lord is their strength, they wouldn't be able to whip a sick rabbit.

Gripers are also discouraging to be around. They say things like, "Nice suit. Too bad they didn't have your size." Or, "Great dress. Do you think that will be coming back into style?" One lady told me she never understood suffering until she heard me speak. Some people bring joy wherever they go; gripers bring joy whenever they go. When you see them coming, you wish you had an "invisible pill."

Encouraging negative people to be positive can get very interesting. You tell them not to say things like "I will not succeed, I will not succeed," but to say something positive. Then they come back with, "I will fail, I will fail." Now they are not only negative, but they are also positively negative. They see the grapes, but they would rather gripe. You can't talk negative people into being positive. It isn't the facts; it's their focus. Focus is like gathering evidence. Some gather for the prosecution, and others gather for the defense. What I have discovered is most people rarely switch sides. They rise and whine and then wonder why their life is a wilderness experience.

Here's one more question. Is the land you walk on called "The Promised Land" or should it be called "Belly Acres"?

Rise and Shine

A man lived on the border between Wisconsin and Minnesota. He had assumed that he lived in Minnesota, but a new survey showed that he actually lived in Wisconsin. "Thank goodness," he exclaimed, "I never could bear those cold Minnesota winters."

Thank goodness it is possible to rise and shine. There is always a group that comes back with grapes instead of gripes. These are the people that wake up singing, "Oh what a beautiful morning." They rise and shine. If they were football players, they would signal for a great catch instead of a fair catch. They know that their outlook influences the outcome.

I heard a story about a doctor who was making rounds in a ward of terminally ill patients. He asked each of them whether he or she had any final requests. To one older lady, he said, "Is there anything you especially want before you pass on?" She replied, "Yes, I'd like to see my immediate family one more time." "Of course," said the doctor, "we'll arrange it." He asked a second patient for his wishes. "I'm a Catholic," murmured the man. "I'd like to see a priest for confession and last rites." "Certainly," replied the doctor. Then he approached the third patient, "Have you any last wish, sir?" he inquired. "Yes," gasped the old man. "My last wish is to see another doctor." Research on people with life-threatening illnesses suggests that this gentleman just might get well. His focus is on living instead of dying.

Focus is a discipline. To rise and shine, we discipline ourselves to focus on the gains instead of the pains. We focus on what we have learned to focus on. Grandpa and Grandma had the grandchildren for the weekend. They decided to go on a trip. While on the way they noticed a sign that said, "Natural Park" and decided to stop. Grandpa and Grandma were thinking things like nature trails and so forth. But they soon realized that the "Natural Park" was a nudist community – naked people, or, to be politically correct, clothing optional lifestyle. They were appalled, of course, and worried about the children seeing such a thing. But before they could turn around, a group of people came riding by on bicycles. The kids noticed the people and immediately their eyes got big and then one blurted out, "Look, they don't have on their safety helmets." Why would that be their focus? Because they had been taught all their lives never to ride a bicycle without a safety helmet.

A new driver for an interstate trucking company found the long cross-country trips extremely tiring. But he noticed that one of the older drivers he traveled with seemed to thrive on the road. He always looked as fresh at the end of the ride as he did at the start. So one day the young man asked the older one what his secret was. "It's all in your attitude," he replied. "Whereas you went to work this morning, I went for a ride in the country." Your focus will determine if life is a lot of work or a ride in the country.

Focusing on the good takes discipline, but it will make you a positive person. We live in a world that focuses on the negative. Our world doesn't work on a positive basis, so you have to work hard to be a positive person.

Focusing on God takes faith, and faith in God will make us powerful persons. Even when life is difficult, we'll have faith that God has the power to transform messes into miracles and blunders into blessings. When there is no visible evidence to be positive, then discipline can lead us to faith. We believe that even in the worst situations, God can bring about good.

When people and situations have power over us, we pity ourselves and whine. When God has power over us, we pity the whiners and shine. Therefore, our uplook (faith) makes us powerful and affects our outlook (attitude), which makes us positive and affects our outcome (life), which allows us to rise and shine.

Just Say No, I Mean Yes

There is no such thing as self-control. Do you realize you can't "not" do anything? The more you try "not to do," the worse it gets. The moment I'm on a diet, I think about Twinkies and Snickers, even when I'm not hungry. When I think about not eating, all I think about is the food I want to eat. You can't "not" do anything.

For example, just imagine that an elephant in pink pajamas and yellow roller skates is rolling along beside you right now. Picture the funny looking elephant. Can you see it? Now, get the elephant out of your mind. You don't see it any more. It's not gone? No? You still see it? The best way to remove the image of the elephant is to replace it with something else – perhaps a zebra in blue pajamas. You see, putting off (stopping) something is temporary unless you put on (start) something else.

Let's say you come to my house and tell me, "Charles, this furniture is junk. It's late attic, early Sears – it's awful. You need to get rid of this junk." I say, "I know. I hate this chair and that table is pitiful. Will you help me get rid of it?" You say, "Yes, I have a pickup truck. Let's load it up and take it to the dump." We load it up, take it to the dump, and I come back home and think, "Thanks, I feel better getting rid of all that junk." I'm a little tired but there is no chair to sit on. It's at the dump. I'd rather sit on the floor than in that chair. I'm hungry and there's no table, but I'd rather eat on the floor than that pitiful table. I may sit and eat on the floor for a little while, but if I don't replace the furniture soon, I'll be right back at the dump getting the same old junk.

Years ago, one national campaign that was against drugs ran on this slogan: "Just say no." The problem is, that's impossible. In order to say "no" to something, you have to say "yes" to something else. There's no such thing as self-control. You can't erase unless you replace. Have you had a vacant lot in your neighborhood? What did it look like? I think I can tell you. It was the trashiest place in the neighborhood because vacant lots attract trash, and so do vacant lives.

Our tendency is to go through life trying *not* to do things. We make up more rules and regulations for what we can't do instead of focusing on what we can do. We become narrow, negative, nauseating and, well – *vacant*.

Today, think of something you can say "yes" to. Don't say "yes" to just anything, like the single girl who answered the phone, "Yes, yes, I'll marry you – who is this?" Say "yes" to something that will improve your vacant life.

A desperate girl was tired of living so she jumped off a bridge. A man saw her and jumped in to save her, forgetting he couldn't swim. As he began to thrash and scream, she swam over and pulled him to shore. She went from tired of living to being excited about life; from giving up to helping out; from being destroyed to being developed. She went from being blasted by life to being blessed by life. Why? She found something to say "yes" to.

Go out there and jump off a bridge (symbolically speaking, of course). Find something to say "yes" to. Your lot in life is beginning to look better already.

The Blame Game

It started with the first family. Adam blamed Eve. Eve blamed the serpent. And of course the serpent didn't have a leg to stand on. The problem, of course, was not the apple in the tree; it was the pair on the ground. (Also, Adam provided a valuable lesson for humanity that a man should never forget – never make a big decision when talking to a naked woman.)

Our family played the blame game. Our first born, Angela, was an only child for the first five years of her life, so we always knew who did it – she did. Then the second came along, and of course Angela passed it on to Kasey, who was always to blame because she couldn't talk. Then Kasey passed it on to Breanne who was always guilty because she couldn't defend herself. When they could all talk, they claimed they didn't know who did it. Then they said the gremlins did it.

Kids have a hard time taking responsibility. When a kid comes home late, he never says he stopped at Bobby's, started playing, and just forgot to come home. Instead, he claims he had to stop and help some elderly lady cross the street. It's always something noble.

How many times have you heard a child tell the truth about why his homework isn't done? You never hear, "I didn't get it done because I'm lazy," or "I watched too much television." Yeah right! They come up with things like "I was running a fever of almost 105° and could hardly raise my head up." *Clubhouse Magazine* had a contest which asked kids to send in the best excuse they'd ever given for not doing their homework. One boy said, "I went on a hot air balloon ride, and we were going to crash because there was too much weight in the basket. I threw my homework out, and it saved our lives."

Unfortunately the blame game continues into adulthood. During most of my counseling sessions, people would try to explain their behavior. I asked, "Why did you act that way?" They responded, "I lost my head." I said, "Wow, where did you get that replacement? It fits so well." Or they said, "I was just beside myself." I'd ask, "Could you do that for me?" Another explanation was, "I lost my temper." I told them, "You mean you found your temper." They also claimed, "All my problems are caused by someone else." I eventually learned to say, "I don't counsel people who aren't here. It keeps me sane."

Of course, when I was inexperienced I empathized and got involved. One wife told me her husband was awful, called her names, and locked her in the basement. I said, "He locked you in the basement? What a jerk." He was scheduled to come in the next day, and that night I thought he must be a gorilla. Then a nice guy showed up, clothed, and in his right mind and told me the other side of the story – what his wife had said and what she had done. No wonder he locked her in the basement! That's where she belonged.

I discovered that everyone has a side. I heard his side and her side, the kid's side, the parent's side and even told my side a time or two. Lately, even computers have a side. What really matters is God's side. I would like to tell you His story. His story is that we've been redeemed and we can re-dream, no matter what the circumstances. Since we live in a fallen world, our image of God has been defaced but not erased. No matter what has been done to us, it can't defeat us unless we allow it to. With God's power we can climb on the rocks thrown at us.

Whatever the problem, shortcoming, mistake, excuse, disaster, or weakness, we can always play the blame game and find a gremlin to pin it on. But it doesn't matter if you did it, they did it, or the computer did it. The only thing that matters is how you respond to it.

When people and situations have power over you, you blame, shame, call people names, and remain the same. You blame people, pity yourself, and end up miserable. When you realize that God has power over situations and people, you thank God and pity people.

God gives us many gifts, but one of the most powerful is response-ability. This is the ability to respond in a way that is good for us. No one can change the past, but you can begin now to take responsibility for your future.

Happy Landing

I'm not afraid of flying; I'm afraid of crashing. I have traveled for many years and have been in more hotel rooms than Gideon's Bible. Usually, I was speaking at churches. That meant cheap hotels (you know the kind where you have to put a quarter in the bed to keep it from vibrating) and cheap airfares. That means you fly first class only if you are baggage. What is the deal about first class anyway? It's always in the front. Have you ever heard of an airplane backing into a mountain? So I don't mind not being in first class.

Flying on a small airline is what really bothers me – the kind where the pilot does everything: loads your baggage, takes the tickets, then puts on his goggles and scarf and welcomes you on his plane. Of course, the airline really has two pilots – Wilbur, your pilot, and his brother, Orville, who is on vacation.

One plane I was on was so small that it had a luggage rack on the back and a bug screen on the front windshield. It was like getting into Christmas wrapping paper. It made me nervous, and I thought about airplane poison: one drop will kill you. I got hold of myself. I tried to think positively. I'm close to the "home office" up there – well, sort of close; the cruising altitude was only 2200 feet. I thought biblical thoughts – faith, hope, and gravity, I mean charity. I listened for the pilot to give his spiel about cabin depressurization and oxygen masks, but instead I heard Wilbur say, "If this thing drops real fast, there is a Bible under your seat and a copy of Evelyn Woods' Speed Reading Course." I confessed sins I had just thought about doing. I would have buckled my seat belt, but I didn't have one. At least we had a roll bar on top. We took off and it was interesting. The pilot's wife sent some homemade cookies, and his son showed slides of their vacation. I started to get more comfortable and decided to read. I turned on the reading light and the plane slowed down. I got nervous again. It was bumpy. We stopped three times en route; two were to ask for directions. We did a little crop dusting on the way, and finally we landed.

I did get home. Now that I look back on it, that's what really matters. The take-offs and landings came out even, and I got home. As I think about life, getting home is also what matters. As God's children, heaven is our home, and He promises us a happy landing.

Children sum up theology so well. A little boy got to go pick out a puppy for his birthday. Out of a whole litter of puppies he picked one of the smaller, nondescript dogs. His father, somewhat surprised, asked why he picked that one. He said, "It's wagging its tail. I want the one with the happy ending."

Life is like a flight on a small airline. It can be very interesting, but it is also bumpy and sometimes a little scary. Make sure you have the right pilot for a happy landing (or should I say ending) and enjoy the flight.

Be Possible

The Rolling Stones sand a song that said, "Time is on my side." Then the backup singers would chime in, "Yes, it is, yes, it is." Well, I want to tell you that time is not on your side. No it isn't, no it isn't. If you don't believe it, look at your stomach. Everything is headed south. The fact is that, in dog years, most of us are already dead.

I heard about a clock that was advertised as the perfect gift idea. When you punched in your age and your gender, the digital clock would constantly remind you of how many more years you could expect to live. It displayed your remaining time (based on life-expectancy tables) in hours, minutes, and seconds. This clock would tell you exactly, down to the last second, how much time you had left. But the clock is a hoax because no one knows how long he or she has left.

Whatever you need to do – do it now. A boy and a girl returned to the girl's home after their first date. Standing at the front door, the boy asked nervously, "May I kiss you?" There was no reply. Again he asked, "May I kiss you?" No reply. A third time he asked, "May I kiss you?" Still no reply. "Are you deaf?" asked the boy. "Are you paralyzed?" the girl replied.

Sometimes you just need to do something. Make an effort and decide to do it now, not later. A boat in a harbor is safe, but, in time, the bottom will rot out. If you just sit, pardon the bluntness, your bottom is going to rot out. Get on with it. Your favorite song should not be "Sittin' on the Dock of the Bay." "One of these days" too easily becomes "none of these days."

A teacher asked her students what they wanted to become when they grew up. A chorus of responses came from all over the room. "A football player." "A doctor." "An astronaut." "The President." "A fireman." "A teacher." "A race car driver." Every one had an answer except one little boy named Johnny. The teacher noticed that Johnny was just sitting there quiet and still, so she asked, "Johnny, what do you want to be when you grow up?" "Possible," Johnny replied. "Possible?" asked the teacher. "Yes," Johnny said, "My mom is always telling me I'm impossible. So when I grow up, I want to be possible."

Everything is possible today. Do it today. You can't promise you'll do it tomorrow; just say you'll do it today. Maybe you didn't do it yesterday, but you can do it today because today it is possible. Whatever you're struggling with, you can do it today. "Today I will be a great marriage partner." "Today I will not overeat." "Today I will not criticize." Whatever it is, today you can do it.

The best way to live life is to live it in the present. Take it a day at a time. You might have heard about the young clock that got a little stressed out. He began to think introspectively about how many times he had to tick. He had to tick two times for every second. That's 120 ticks per minute. Then he took it further. That's 7,200 ticks in an hour. That's over 172,000 ticks a day and over 1.2 million ticks in a week. Overwhelmed by all the ticking he became stressed and depressed. So he went to see the clock psychiatrist. He told the psychiatrist how many ticks he had to tick and wondered how he was going to do this. The clock psychiatrist rubbed his numerals and wisely asked, "Young clock, how many ticks do you tick at a time?" The clock responded, "Just one." The clock doctor said, "Then that is what you have to focus on. Tick one tick at a time, or you'll be ticked off the rest of your life."

That's the way it is with you and me. When I was growing up I sang one solo in church my entire life. I was eight years old, and my dad was the pastor. A bunch of kids decided we wanted to sing a song, and he let us do it. We sang "It Is No Secret What God Can Do." After I finished, one church lady said, "It wasn't as bad as it sounded." That ended my singing career but I remember the words to the song. "It is no secret what God can do. What He's done for others, He'll do for you."

It is possible. I don't know what your past is, I don't know what your future will be, but I can tell you that with God's help, today is possible.

Turning Over the Keys

Finding Forrester is a great movie. Sean Connery plays the part of a legendary writer who mentors a young man who has great potential as a writer. Connery tells Forrester to sit at the typewriter and begin typing – just type what comes to mind. Just start.

Think of five frogs sitting on a log. One decides to jump off. How many frogs are left? Five. Thinking of jumping and actually jumping are two different things. Lots of people come to church on Sunday and decide to change, but they never make the change. It is difficult to go from awareness to action. The problem is trust.

A construction crew was putting a drain line in a building. A power cable was directly in the path of their work. Construction stopped while an electrician was called who declared that there was no electrical power to the cable. The foreman asked, "Are you sure the power is dead to the cable and there is no danger?" "Absolutely," replied the electrician. "Well then, you cut the line." After a pause, the electrician said, "I'm not that sure." Most of us don't take action because we're not that sure. We are not that sure we can trust God.

Turning over control of your life is tough. It's like driving. You give the keys to your car to someone else and turn total control of your car to her. If you know and trust her it's easy. And what about riding with your teenager for the first time? I have done this three times with three girls. I taught my daughter, Angela, to drive in Dallas. It's pretty scary riding with a teenager in Dallas. The first time she drove, we went only around the block. I tried to drive the car from the passenger seat. "No! Don't do that! Slow down! There's a stop sign! Watch out for that car!" The more I shouted, the more stressed she got. I'm hollering at her and she's hollering back at me. It was a miserable ride. Finally we were back at the house; we had made it around the block. Our driveway had an iron gate that was just big enough for a car to fit through. As she pulled in, I was thinking I should tell her, "Don't hit the gate. Don't hit the gate." But then I thought, "I've been griping about the way she drives the whole time. I'm not going to say anything about the gate; I'm just going to be quiet." I kept quiet and she hit the gate. She was in her mother's car – I didn't trust her in mine.

We often do the same thing with God. We give God the keys to our lives but then we try to stay in control, "Wait! Don't you see that? Stop! Slow down!" I gripe and mumble and complain and get stressed out. It becomes a miserable ride. Then I go eat a Snickers or ice cream. I have started a vicious cycle. The problem is a lack of trust. I need to learn to trust God.

Let's say that you have a chance to win five million dollars. All you have to do is drive in the Indianapolis 500. You have to finish, but not win the race, to receive the money. You are a little worried, but then Al Unser says he'll drive the car for you. All you have to do is give him the keys. If he finishes, you get the money. What are you going to do? If you have any sense you give the keys to Al without a second thought. The amazing thing is that most of us won't do that in a practical situation. In essence, we say, "Well, Al, I think I'm going to do it myself. I know that I've never raced before, and I've never driven over 75 mph, but I think I can do it. I think I can finish." You'd say, "You're nuts!"

What's the bottom line? God drives better than Al; give Him the keys.

7

Personal Belief

This last chapter is about the greatest story ever told. If you're not a follower of Christ, let me warn you that this chapter is about my personal faith. Skip it if you must, but for me, it is this old story that makes all the other stories possible and powerful.

A Great House

After being away on business, a man thought it would be nice to bring his wife a little gift. "How about some perfume?" he asked the cosmetics clerk. She showed him a bottle costing $75. "That's a bit much," he said, so she returned with a smaller bottle for $50. "That's still quite a bit," the man complained. Growing annoyed, the clerk brought out a tiny $20 bottle. "What I mean is I'd like to see something really cheap," the man said. The clerk handed him a mirror. I've known people like that. Many are heads of finance departments.

Thank goodness God is not cheap. An elderly, wealthy lady was sitting in her Mercedes waiting for a parking place at the grocery store. She had been waiting patiently as a car backed out. Just as the car pulled out, a young man whizzed right in and took the place. He got out of the car and, as he walked to the store, he said to the lady, "That is what you can do when you're young and quick." She took her Mercedes and smashed the back of his car over and over. He ran up to her screaming, "Lady, what are you doing? Are you crazy? That's my car." She calmly said, "That's what you can do when you're old and rich."

God is ageless and rich, but He uses His riches for us, for our benefit. I'm not talking about material riches. Many things are more important than money.

A desperate old prospector in Deadwood, South Dakota, inscribed this saying on a weathered piece of wood: "I lost my gun, I lost my horse, I am out of food, the Indians are after me, but I have all the gold I can carry." Here is a guy who didn't understand that some things are more important than gold.

A humorous story is told about the golfer, Arnold Palmer. Palmer was invited to play a series of exhibition golf matches in Saudi Arabia. The king of Saudi Arabia was so impressed with Arnie, and so appreciative of Palmer's impact on his countrymen, that he wanted to give him a gift. "It really isn't necessary," Palmer insisted. "I am honored to have been invited." The king was persistent. "I would be unhappy if I could not show you my appreciation," he said. Finally, Arnie relented. He thought for a moment and said, "Well, how about a golf club? That would make a nice memento of my visit to your country." The next day Arnold Palmer received the title to a golf club – consisting of thousands of acres of real estate, a clubhouse, beautiful trees, etc.

The king did not give out of his riches; he gave according to his riches. That is what God does for us. God can do more than you can even think about doing. God can give you more than you can ever think about wanting. God is able to give you more than you are able to ask or think. Here is our problem. We put God in our sphere and expect Him to operate as we do.

It's like the loan officer who worked at a bank. He did a great job, and when he retired he decided to run a gas station. The business was a horrible failure because, when customers asked for ten gallons of gas, he asked if they would settle for five. What he was used to doing didn't work in retail. What we are used to doesn't apply to God.

Believe it or not, I can lift an object that weighs a ton. I would need to be in outer space to do it, for there is no gravity out there. It's a whole different sphere. I have power there that I don't have here.

God is in a different sphere. He doesn't operate the way our puny minds operate. He is God. He can do more abundantly than what we can ever ask or think. The issue is confidence.

When our oldest daughter turned fifteen, the state of Texas believed that she would be competent to drive. That would not have bothered me if the state of Texas had decided she could drive a state vehicle. That would be their problem. However, they thought that she could drive, at age fifteen, in *my* vehicle. I loved Angela, but I didn't really trust her driving. I didn't think she was really competent. I had a hard time giving her the keys to the car. I'd say, "Today why don't you drive around the neighborhood." Or maybe on a Sunday, when there was not much traffic, I would let her drive to church. I didn't want her out in the real world. I had a problem trusting her competence.

That's the way some of us think about God. We think God is with us, but we're not going to give Him the keys. We don't want Him to go out in the real world; we just want him to stay in the neighborhood or maybe at church, but not in the real world. We don't want God to dominate us. Don't be so naive as to think that you aren't dominated by something. People say they just want to be free. You can say you want to be free from brushing your teeth. You will be free from the toothbrush, but you will be dominated by cavities. Life involves choices, and it's always a choice as to who or what will dominate us. When we say that a person is filled with anger, what we mean is that that person is dominated by anger. Sooner or later, anger will come out. When God dominates you, He soon comes out.

A wealthy man's foreman was extremely helpful. When the man decided to take a vacation he told the foreman, "Build a house that is wonderful. Spare no expense on materials and construction. I will be gone for six months, and when I return I want the keys to the house." The foreman started the house and soon realized that if he used substandard materials he could pocket the extra money. And that's what he did. The house was a second-rate house built with second-rate materials. When the wealthy man returned he asked for the keys to the house. "Did you build me a great house?" "Yes," the foreman replied. "Did you use the finest materials?" "Yes," he again replied. His boss said, "Great, because this house is for you," and he handed him the keys.

We have a wealthy God who spares no expense. Let Him build you a great house.

Lessons Learned at the Grocery Store

Have you ever thought what it's like to be a kid at the grocery store? Mother is rushing, and she takes the kid and stuffs him into the steel seat and says, "Sit there and be quiet. I've got to pick up a couple of things." Now when mother says "a couple of things" that means a couple of things from each section.

"Now, son," she says, "you can't have anything. Just sit there and be quiet. I will roll you up and down the aisles, and you can see all the wonderful things to get, but you can't have anything. I will get everything I want, and not only that, you will have to sit on what I get." Well, to a kid that's like sitting on McDonald's lap and not getting a Happy Meal. Children are not happy campers in the grocery store.

I have a friend who was with his son in the grocery store. His son kept asking him if he could be a dog. Finally the dad said, "Fine, be a dog. Just leave me alone." Later he saw his son, Jake, run up to a man and lick his leg. Horrified, my friend ran to apologize to the man. The guy took it well and said, "I'm just glad he didn't think I was a fire hydrant."

A lady told me about going grocery shopping with her young son. She was in a hurry so she put her son in the cart and told him to be quiet. As she hurried along, putting stuff in the cart, the kid spotted some chocolate chip cookies. He said, "Mom, please may I have some chocolate chip cookies?" She said, "No! I told you to be quiet." About the fourth aisle the kid asked again if he could have just a few chocolate chip cookies. Again she told him no and to be quiet. About the sixth aisle he asked, "Mom, could I just have *one* chocolate chip cookie?" Again she said no, popped him, and said to hush or she would have the manager put him in the big freezer.

When they got to the check-out line, the line was long. The mother glanced down and saw a gleam in her son's eye. She knew something was coming, but she didn't know what. All of a sudden, the kid stood straight up in his seat, lifted his hand straight toward heaven and in his loudest voice hollered, "In the name of Jesus, give me some chocolate chip cookies!" The place erupted in applause, so he said it again. More applause. The mother didn't know what to do with everyone clapping, so she ran to the shelf and got him the chocolate chip cookies.

Now what can we learn about life in the grocery store? As an adult, I learned that sometimes when I go to the store I get things I don't need and I don't realize how much they cost until I get to the check-out. It's kind of like life. If you live by distraction instead of direction, and don't have a list of priorities to go by, it could be that when it's time to check out you realize some things cost you a whole lot more than you thought they would.

We can learn something important from the little boy in the grocery store. In a simple but powerful way his story teaches us that when you come to the check-out of life with no resources and no hope, you, too, may need a higher power. Maybe you are ready to check out on a relationship. Maybe your feelings are dead. Call on the name of Jesus. This Jesus has been known to bring dead things back to life.

L.O.V.E.

Everyone is talking about love. The Bible says we are to love one another. It sounds good but it seems impossible. Whoever said, "I love mankind; it's the people I can't stand," was right.

A waitress running a cash register got irritated because everyone who walked by asked what time it was. Finally she bought a clock and put it right by her cash register. Then everyone who came by said, "Is that clock right?" People are just aggravating. I had a secretary who never answered the phone. I finally asked her, "Why don't you answer the phone when it rings?" She said, "Why should I? Nine out of ten times it's for you."

It's hard to love others. It's even sometimes difficult to love your own family. One guy told his wife that if she really loved him, she would have married someone else.

Here are some hints on learning to love others:

LISTEN   You can't really love anyone unless you listen. Most of our difficulties are from not listening. Like the old couple rocking on the porch. She turned to her husband and said, "I'm proud of you." He responded, "I'm tired of you, too." Listen not just to the facts, but to the feeling behind the facts.

OVERLOOK   Most things that irritate need to be overlooked. Our tendency is to retaliate. I know I do. A man called me one morning at 3:00 a.m. to tell me my dog was barking. I called him back the next morning at 3:00 a.m. to tell him I didn't have a dog.

One lady came home and found that her teenage son had forgotten to put the clothes in the dryer. She pitched a fit and began preaching a sermon about his irresponsibility. The son, about halfway through the sermon, interrupted and asked, "Mom, when you are at church and a parent says, 'My son is on drugs,' and another says, 'My daughter is pregnant,' and another says her thirteen-year-old son is in reform school, do you say, 'That's nothing, my boy forgets to put the clothes in the dryer?'" Some things we should just overlook.

VALUE   To value people means to acknowledge their true worth. A renowned pastor officiated at many weddings. Often, the nervous groom would ask, "Reverend, how much do I owe you?" The pastor would always smile, look at the groom, and say, "Just pay me what she's worth." He made a lot of money on weddings because, at that point in time, to the groom, this lady was of unbelievable value.

ENCOURAGEMENT   You will never understand human behavior when you're at Six Flags with your child, and you put her on a carousel and then try to go get a cold drink. Every time you try to leave she calls and you have to stay to watch. Why? Because we all have the need to be appreciated.

A little boy asked his dad to throw darts with him. His dad agreed, but after a while he said, "Son, you are throwing all the darts. What am I supposed to do?" He answered, "Dad, I'm supposed to throw the darts and you're supposed to say, 'Wonderful!'" Everyone needs someone to say "Wonderful!" when we are throwing, and especially when we are receiving, the darts of life.

L.O.V.E. – Listen, Overlook, Value, and Encourage. Do that every day and you will love the people around you. The problem is, it's hard to do that every day. Real love is impossible. It is supernatural. We can love only to the extent that we have been loved.

A salesman called his wife from a coin-operated phone in a distant city. After he finished the conversation, he said good-bye and replaced the receiver. As he was walking away, the phone rang. He went back and answered it, expecting to be informed of extra charges. It was the operator and she said, "I thought you'd like to know just after you hung up, your wife said, 'I love you.'"

Even if you have hung up on God, He says "I love you." Reminds me of another person, who after He was hung up, said, "I love you."

Keep It Simple

It's easy to feel stupid these days. I watched *Jeopardy* on TV and didn't know any of the questions to the answers and it made me feel stupid. So I changed the channel and watched *Wheel of Fortune* instead and then felt stupid just for watching it. By the way, watching Vanna White doesn't qualify for spending time with a word processor. While watching *Wheel of Fortune* I noticed that I still haven't programmed my VCR – I got it for Christmas in 1991. I worked on that a while and made some progress. Now it's not flashing 12:00 anymore: it's flashing 4:00. There is nothing good on TV anyway. I should've known that when I hit the TV remote and the trash compactor came on. It's amazing. I have forty-six channels and nothing to watch. It seems like the bigger the screen, the worse the TV programming is.

I don't have time to relax anyway. My staff told me that I have to get on the information highway. I try to do my part. When we go to daylight savings time, I set my alarm for 2:00 a.m. and get up to change the time. It always makes me tired, and then I can't go back to sleep because I'm wondering, if I set my clock forward, will I miss sixty minutes?

I feel like road kill on the informational highway. I was educated differently. In my day, a classroom was high-tech if it had an electrical outlet. Now I'm surrounded by techno-wizards. One guy in my office comes in, holds his watch to the computer screen and it programs his schedule into his watch. I'm his boss and I don't know whether to look into his eyes or talk to his watch.

I have a brand new computer. It's powerful – it has rams, MB's and more buttons to push than I've ever seen. I imagine it as a big TV remote, and my testosterone level starts to rise when I'm in control of this powerful remote. This is great. It's so big I'll never lose it as I do the TV remote. It's so powerful that I can fly into cyberspace. I'm ready to begin my journey from the dirt road to the great informational highway. I have everything I need.

So I sat down and looked at all those keys, and I didn't know how to work any of them – not one. They say, when all else fails, read the instructions, so I started reading the instruction manual but discovered that it's in a foreign language – I think it's called Nerd Latin. There were no jokes, no pictures, and no color-by-number illustrations. I discovered a phone number, so I called a techno-wizard to help me. You know the sequence…if you need so and so, press one, etc. I waited until I got the right menu and it said, "If you are an idiot and have a brand new computer and don't know what any of the keys mean, press 666, or e-mail us at our web site, beast.com." I closed my eyes and pressed the numbers and saw myself arriving in cyberhell.

I heard a pleasant voice. This is how the conversation went: "You could have a virus." "No way – I'm not into computer dating; I'm a married man." Then the questions began. "Have you even booted up?" "No, I just have some loafers." "Do you have new windows?" "No, but we did paint the old ones a few years ago." "Are you in the DOS command?" "No, I'm in my office." "Then you must be working under windows." "No I'm over by the wall, actually close to the table if that makes any difference." "Do you have a mouse?" "Sir, what does the animal kingdom have to do with this?" From there it went to name-calling. I think he called me a Yahoo. I hung up, but I didn't give up.

My staff told me to start with e-mail. I had to learn to communicate, so now I read e-mail. It's really easy. My secretary downloads my e-mail, pushes print, and it shows up on my desk on a piece of paper. Now that's America! What else would we do with all those trees if we didn't make paper? I think I've figured out e-mail. E-mail happens when you let a pigeon into cyberspace. He carries the message from one web site to another. Hence the term – web. Now these cyber pigeons can't understand English because they're animals. The only other animal they understand is a mouse. So you have to have a cyber mouse to communicate your message to the cyber pigeon, and you have to know how to open windows so the pigeon can get out into cyberspace. And of course the more pigeons you have, the more (bytes) you get.

Personally, I like living on the dirt road. It may not be high-tech but it's simple. Never mind that I require at least three other people working on their computers so that I can have Informational power; that's not the point. The point is, I like things simple. I'm a bottom line kind of guy. I guess that's why I like the gospel – it's simple but it's powerful. In a sense, it's like my office. Someone else did the work.

Game Of Life = Finish

The other day I lived out one of my dreams. I played golf at the Colonial Country Club in Fort Worth, Texas, and the management provided me with a caddie. Me, with a caddie. I felt like a real pro. It was a little stressful at the first tee. I took a mighty swing and missed the ball. "This course must be a few inches lower than mine," I said. I took another mighty swing. I missed it again. "Man, this is the toughest course I have ever played," I exclaimed. The caddie said, "Don't quit now; you have a no hitter going." Then I nailed it. It really took off. We couldn't find it. I was furious. "Caddie," I hollered, "aren't you supposed to watch my ball?" "Yes sir," he said, "it just caught me by surprise when you actually hit it."

It got worse. I started slicing like a food processor. Now for those who don't know much about golf, if the golf ball goes to the right, it's a slice; if it goes to the left, it's a hook; and if you hit it straight, it's a miracle. Not many miracles were happening in my game. I took it out on my caddie. I said, "You must be the worst caddie in the world." He said, "No, sir, that would be too much of a coincidence." I asked him why he kept looking at his watch. He said it was a compass he kept checking.

We started the back nine. I had a beautiful short game; unfortunately, it was off the tee. I missed a hole-in-one on a par three by four strokes. I started to swing faster and faster. I swung so fast one guy in my group got whiplash just watching it. We finally got to the eighteenth hole. The caddie said he was going to fly the green flag at half-mast in honor of my game. The caddie was nice. He thanked me. He said he had been a caddie at this course for forty years, but today I showed him parts of this golf course that he had never seen before.

People love golf, and they take it seriously. We let a group play through the other day. One of the group said his wife was in a serious accident, and they were trying to finish as quickly as they could.

What can be learned from golf? It is like life. Someone has said, "You never own a golf swing; you just borrow it." This means that if you stop doing the basic things, you'll end up in trouble pretty quickly. Isn't that true in life? Some basic things you may need to remember. Also, the golf course has many hazards – sand, rough, water, trees, etc. It's best to know where they are and have a plan for avoiding them. Have you been in the sand trap of life lately? Why not develop a plan to stay in the fairway?

We could make other comparisons about golf and life, like the bad break you get when the ball bounces the wrong way. Of course, no sense complaining, you have to play it where it ends up or take a penalty stroke. Some golfers cheat to avoid the consequences, but other golfers don't want to play with them or, if we are talking about life, live with them or work with them.

I've learned a lot playing golf. One thing is to take one hole at a time. Even if you did poorly on the last hole, it doesn't count on the next hole. It sure would be discouraging if golf courses had just one hole, 7,288 yards long. People wouldn't play that course. It would be too discouraging. That's why they have eighteen separate holes. It keeps you trying to do better on the next one. Don't make life one long discouraging event. Set some small specific goals to keep you encouraged in your game of life.

The most important thing I've learned from golf I learned in a scramble tournament. That's when you get to play the best ball. I was paired with a pro. He was so good that I really didn't have to worry about my shots. If I did awful, I could walk up to where he had hit. It was wonderful! I was so relaxed I realized I was playing my best golf.

Trying to be good at golf can cause a lot of stress. It can quickly put you in the "hall of shame." That's probably why Mark Twain said, "Golf is a good walk ruined." When I played in that tournament, I had a designated golfer (the pro). He took the pressure off my performance and enabled me to play up to my potential.

Life is like that. You can get so caught up with the performance of it that you live below your potential. If only we would relax. That's why God sent Jesus (a pro at life) to live a perfect life and to assure you a place in heaven (Hall of Fame). The game of life is different from the game of golf in that it doesn't really matter what you score: it's where you finish. You could remember the difference by saying "GOLF: GAME OF LIFE = FINISH." So next time you play golf or watch it, think about the game of life and your designated pro – Jesus – and your Hall of Fame finish. Then relax, enjoy the scenery, take some good swings, and, like the Apostle Paul (who must have been a golfer), finish the course.

Recycling Your Past

A mailman with a new route came to a house with a mean-looking German shepherd on the porch. When he approached the mailbox, the dog jumped twenty feet in the air, and then sat down. The owner walked out to check on the commotion. The mailman asked in amazement, "Why did he do that?" He replied, "We took his chain off yesterday, and he hasn't realized it." The dog was living in the past.

One time, we bought a two-year-old dog from a classified ad. Unfortunately, when we tried to pet the dog he jumped away. Evidently the dog had been abused and, although we loved him, he wouldn't let us pet him. We raised a hand of love, but because of the past, he saw a hand to be feared. I've discovered that many people live the same way.

A mother looking out her kitchen window saw her children circling a family of skunks. Panicking, she opened the window and called, "Run, run!" Each kid picked up a skunk and ran. Do you feel as if your life is like this? Do you pick up your stinking past and run with it? You might find a new job or a new relationship, but then you pick up your stinking past and run with it.

Vacationing in Italy, a man and his wife took some unforgettable taxi rides through Rome. Although they were seasoned travelers, nothing could have prepared them for the thrill of Roman taxi rides. Few traffic lights slowed them and with no lane stripes on the wide streets, every day is like the Ben Hur Memorial. Cars speed through blind corners and jockey for position while going around traffic circles. If those taxies were at Disney Land, they would be an E-Ticket ride. During one trip the man noticed the cab didn't have a rearview mirror or side mirrors. When he paid the fair, he couldn't resist asking the driver about the mirrors. Twisting in his seat, he said in broken English and with great intensity, "Mister, if you gonna drive in this city, the first thing you gotta learn is this: whassa behinda you isa *not* important!"

That's life. If you're going to drive the car of life, you need to realize that "whassa behinda you isa not important." You must look ahead. On either ESPN or ESPN2 or ESPN Forever, I saw a car race where all the cars drive backwards. They have to go backwards to win the race. The cars were banged up from constantly running into each other. That's how it is with a lot of people. They drive backwards, but God says you will never be what He wants you to be by driving backwards.

Our past is like garbage – you have to take it out. You can't move it to the garage and leave It, which I've been known to do. The garage is like your subconscious. You can put it there, but if you have enough garbage in the garage it will eventually stink up the house. Not only that, someone has to take it away. That's what God does. He not only takes it away, but He also recycles it. I don't recycle very much because of all the sorting. God doesn't make us sort; we just give it to Him. He recycles it and gives it back as a blessing. Remember what the world wants to bury you with, God can bless you with.

An angry owner took his frustration out on his hard-working horse by throwing it in the trash dump to die. He had his crew pour trash on him every hour to bury him alive. The horse shook off the trash and stomped on it. Each time he did this he rose a little higher. After the third day he was free. I'm not saying that you won't have trash dumped on you, but that God is able to take it and turn it into a treasure.

A particular salesman was very good at selling vacuum cleaners. His technique was to dump dirt all over the client's furniture and carpet and then vacuum the dirt and make a sale. His sales manager sent him into the rural areas where he used the same technique. At a remote farmhouse he spread dirt all over the floor and furniture and asked the farmer for the nearest outlet. The farmer said, "Sorry, son, we don't have electricity in this room." This man had a lot of dirt and no power. Many people have a lot of dirt in their lives with no power to get rid of it. God gives us the power to get rid of the dirt and the hurt. He knows you have scars. We all have scars.

A single guy arrived at work with scars on both his ears. A friend asked what happened. He said, "It was terrible. I was ironing my shirt, the phone rang, and I picked up the iron instead of the phone." "That's awful," said his friend, "What happened to the other ear?" The man said, "The guy called back." We need to learn from our scars and not do the same dumb things over and over again. If you look closely at my left eye you'll see a scar. I was five years old and my older brothers were playing baseball. John told me not to walk up while he was hitting the ball. I walked up, and he hit me in the eye with the baseball bat. Eleven stitches later, I knew I would never do that again.

We need to learn from our past but not live there. Move on and realize that Jesus had scars. Thomas asked if He really was the Messiah. Jesus showed him the scars. You'll carry your scars for the rest of your life, but they can be used for good. Since Jesus had scars, He can handle yours. That means the hurt and the dirt can be good, just as the cross was good. What do you do with your scars? Because Jesus came out of the hole His enemies put Him in, you can also have the power to stomp on the dirt and walk out. Remember, what the world wants to bury you with, God wants to bless you with.

Why Do You Think They Call It Labor?

As you read this story I want you to go through a little exercise with me. Put both hands up in the air...higher, there that's better. Your elbow should be next to your ears. Hold them there and continue to read.

You know raising children is not going to be easy if it all starts with something called labor. Sometimes a woman will endure as many as fifteen hours or more of labor to have a baby. However, it's no piece of cake for the men either. Remember, we are the ones in the waiting room with our in-laws for those same fifteen hours, and there is no epidural for that. After the birth occurs, you bring home the perfect Gerber baby. Then reality sets in and you realize you are responsible for another human, and the labor continues. This "perfect" baby throws up at both ends and is totally dependent on you. You feel unprepared like John Kennedy, for example. He sat down in the Oval Office, glanced up at the men who had helped put him there, and said, "Now what are we going to do?" Don't worry; there will be plenty to do. At first you are mostly just cleaning up and feeding. Feeding is the process of putting the fruit on top of the vegetables in the spoon and sticking it in before the baby realizes that he just had his liquid broccoli. Cleaning is the process of.... Well, let's skip that. It's kind of a dirty subject.

The labor increases when the baby learns to talk. And then the questions come. Questions like, "What is God's last name? Does God have a dog? What do batteries run on?" The older the baby gets the more difficult the questions, like, "If dry ice melts, could we go swimming in it and not get wet?" Kids ask strange questions and do strange things like flipping Alka Seltzer into the bathtub water. Their brains have not matured yet, so their bodies suffer the consequences.

Children live in a world that they have to see, feel, and touch to understand. Just listen to a kid when he says abstract words like "I pledge allegiance to the flag." He won't say that. He doesn't know what a pledge or an allegiance is. He will say, "I lead the pigeons to the flag" or something like that. Listen when they say "One nation indivisible." Do you think they say that? No. They don't know what a nation is. They'll say, "One naked individual." They've seen one of those before. Theological concepts are very difficult for kids. They think God's name is Howard because the Bible says "Howard be thy name." Or Art, because the Bible says, "Who art in heaven."

Listen to what kids sing in church. You may be singing, "Soon and very soon, we are going to see the King." They will be singing, "Soon and very soon, we are going to Burger King." One little guy got it all confused and said, "Round John Virgin was the fattest of the twelve opossums." Children can't relate to your adult world. You tell them you have to work late or bring work home that you didn't finish, and they tell you to ask the teacher to put you in a slower group.

Okay, you can put your hands down now. I just wanted you to experience what it's like for a three-year-old to go to the mall with his or her parents. One parent takes one arm, the other takes the other arm, and the kid walks around in pain with you as you tell him this is quality family time.

You find out quickly that the labor is not over at childbirth. The labor continues because it is a sacrifice to enter the child's world. It is eating a pretend meal on plastic plates and reading *The Poky Little Puppy* for the one thousand two hundred fifty fourth time (I think I really did read it that many times, too). Many times the labor leaves you tired, drained, and discouraged. There is something you need to do when this happens. When you are in a discouraging hole, refresh your soul. Remember that you have a perfect Father who entered your world. The one who could eat angel food cake came into our world where the cows eat – in a manger. And when you think of the labor that it takes to enter into a child's world, remember that His labor did not stop at His birth but continued to His death. Jesus, the judge of life, was put on trial. He says that when you are tired of labor, come to Him and He will give you rest.

Remember God entered into our world. It was a labor of love. His hands too were raised high; however, his hands were not held by nails but by love.

Friday's Mess Becomes Sunday's Miracle

It's Friday but Sunday is coming. Only a pastor can relate to those words in terms of sermon preparation. It's Friday and right now nothing is coming for Sunday. I'm a psychologist, but I'm supposed to preach the sermon. I've tried to find a sermon on the internet, and I kept booting up in the wrong shoes and browsing in the wrong rooms. I looked in my files under "sacred," even "top sacred," and I came up empty. I have one great illustration but no sermon to go with it. Rick Warren, a friend of mine, has a purpose for his whole church; I can't even find a purpose for my sermon. When I call "dial-a-prayer," I get the wrong number. Things aren't looking good for a great Sunday.

But I have to deliver a sermon. I'm God's mailman. He's counting on me to deliver His message, and this generation won't listen unless it's first class with their name on it. Right now this sermon may be delivered Bulk Rate for any occupant.

I might need to preach one of those "Hell Fire" sermons. If I can't get them to see the light, surely I can get them to feel the heat. I need a snappy title, something like "Turn or Burn," "Fly or Fry," "Sanctified or French Fried." This isn't working. Maybe I could preach "The Sermon on Amount" and tell them to give all their money.

The last time I preached, the worship leader said I preached a "Long Horn" sermon. It had a point at each end with a lot of bull in the middle. It's easy for him to be critical. He doesn't have to write his material. All he has to do is sing someone else's stuff. I took it like the spiritual man that I am and told him his song wasn't as bad as it sounded. A lady told me once my singing was as bad as it sounded. He told me I wasn't as ugly as I looked.

Well, Sunday comes, ready or not. I managed to come up with a sermon with one point and I finished on time, which is crucial. Remember, those who finish in a flash will last.

It probably wasn't my best sermon; I made a few mistakes. Without realizing it, half way through the sermon I started calling Samson "Tarzan" and of course my dramatic closing line of, "Do you want to end up like Tarzan?" wasn't very effective.

It bothered me a lot, so over lunch Penny and I talked about it. She had some good advice, "Forget the sermon, Charles. Trust me, the congregation already has."

Then it happens. I start the next week and meet someone who tells me that what I said in my sermon changed his or her life. I start to feel proud and think to myself, "Maybe that sermon was good. Maybe it did have a purpose. Maybe Rick Warren will ask me to help him with his next book." I ask, "Exactly what point of mine changed your life?" It was probably that great illustration. The person tells me and I can't believe it. That isn't what I said. It's good, but I didn't say it. When I was younger I used to correct people and try to convince them that I didn't say what they thought I said. Now I just say, "Thank you, I'm glad you were encouraged." Why do I accept their compliment? Because even though I delivered junk mail, they received it as first class and personal with their name on it. It's not like Ed McMahon showed up at their house, but they heard a still, small voice.

It all goes back to Friday and Sunday. Friday's dead message becomes Sunday's live message. Friday's mess becomes Sunday's miracle. What they heard was God. God used what I said to meet their needs. I don't understand it all. Every time I talk about how God uses me I remember the donkey in the Old Testament. It's unexplainable.

It's like the little boy who caught some lightning bugs. His mother asked how they light up like that, and he said, "God does it." She asked, "How does God do it?" The boy thought about that for a minute and then said with confidence, "Remote control, of course."

Well, I don't know how He does it either. It's a little scary, like that first Easter when He made Friday's mess Sunday's miracle. So in the panic of Friday, don't forget the power of Sunday, and thank God for remote control.

More Power to You

When the Pope visited Colorado he was anxious to get to an important meeting. The car assigned to pick him up arrived on time and off they went. The Catholic driver knew that it was the Holy Father riding in the car, so he didn't dare go over the speed limit. However the Pope, anxious to get to the meeting on time, told the driver to pull over and get in the back seat and let him drive. The Holy Father put the pedal to the metal and traveled 85 mph on the Colorado Interstate. Almost immediately a state trooper hiding off the side of the road turned on his siren and lights and gave chase. Catching the speeding car, he ordered the driver to step out. He couldn't believe what he saw and immediately called his captain. He said, "I really got a big one today." The captain said, "You mean the district attorney?" "No sir, much bigger than that." "You have a senator?" came the puzzled reply. "No sir, you don't understand. This is the top of the line." "Who do you have? The President?" "No sir, please understand me; this is something really big." "For heaven's sake, who have you pulled over?" "Well, Captain, I'm not sure, but the Pope is his chauffeur."

That's like Easter. Most people think it's really big, but they just don't know why. I can understand how they could be confused. Did you ever think that the customs surrounding Easter are truly bizarre? First, there is the Easter Bunny, a big male rabbit that carries a nest of eggs. Yes, rabbits are extremely good at carrying out the mandate "be fruitful and multiply," and eggs are perfect, encapsulated symbols of new life to come, but rabbits don't lay eggs or make nests, especially male rabbits. It's enough to confuse adults. No wonder kids have a hard time understanding it.

One little boy said he knew that Jesus died when he went to hang the power lines. The teacher said, "What do you mean?" He handed her a picture. The teacher looked at the picture of Jesus carrying a cross, and it looked just like the utility poles in the little boy's yard. He assumed Jesus worked for the electric company. The teacher explained that the picture was of Jesus dying. He'd combined the ideas, thinking Jesus died when He was hanging power lines. That's not bad theology because, when He died and came back, He gave us resurrection power. He died hanging a power line from God to you.

Preachers are notorious about saying the wrong thing. I heard about one preacher who was trying to establish a good rapport with an inmate about to be executed by the electric chair. The day of the execution came and the pastor was anxious to say just the right words. He thought "goodbye" seemed trite and "see you later" seemed a little inappropriate. As the inmate started to leave, the pastor said, not thinking, "More power to you." Easter is when God gave the power to us, the power to answer the grave question of life. Pardon my pun.

I knew a man who had a trusty old pickup. He told the undertaker he wanted to be buried with his old pickup. The undertaker said, "Why would you want that?" The man said, "I've never seen a hole that this pickup couldn't get me out of." Well, there's one hole your pickup won't get you out of. It's called the grave. You need more power than a pickup to have a good ending to the grave question.

When I started speaking, my dad, who had been preaching for over thirty years at the time, gave me some good advice. He said, "Charles, work on your beginning because it gets people's attention. Don't work too hard on the middle because, whatever you say, people will forget anyway. And, Charles, don't ever forget this: make sure you always have a good ending, because that's what people will remember when they leave." That's Easter. It's the power to have a good ending.

A little girl told her mother she had written a letter to God. "Dear God, instead of letting people die and having to make new ones, why don't you keep the ones that you have now? Love, Alice." She didn't know that God had answered her letter. Easter is when God decided to keep us for eternity. So more power to you.

That's Nuts

Most of us are addicted to something. Some of us are addicted to coffee. *You Know You Are Drinking Too Much Coffee When....* You answer the door before the doorbell rings. You have converted your car's radiator to brew a pot on the way to work. Juan Valdez names his donkey after you. You can play ping-pong without a partner. Your coffee filters are monogrammed. You chew on other people's fingernails. Your eyes stay open even when you sneeze. You can jump start your car without cables. You can photograph yourself from ten feet away without a timer. You ski uphill.

The 12-step program is an interesting program that started many years ago. Rumor has it that Al Gore invented the 12-step program, but that isn't true. It is a program that will help you become the person that God created you to be. People often think that when you become a Christian your problems disappear. That is a myth. When you accept Christ, your personality remains the same, your body remains the same, your bank account remains the same, your habits remain the same, your kids and spouse remain the same, and your friends remain the same. In a sense, we are all in a stage of recovery. You may not need this material, but perhaps you can use this information to help other people.

Two men in a bar noticed that another man kept falling off his stool. Apparently he was so drunk that he couldn't sit on his stool. Being good Samaritans, they offered to take him home. They dragged him to the door and placed him in the car. He fell down three times on the way to the car. When they got him to his house, he fell down four times on the way to the door. They finally made it to the porch and rang the doorbell. When his wife answered the door, they told her they had brought her husband home. She said, "Great – where's his wheelchair?" That was unhelpful and harmful. They didn't know enough to help in the right way.

We cannot be the person God intended us to be unless we ask God to take control. In recovery, the word "real" comes before the word "heal." We have to face it before we can fix it. Without facing it, we will fake it. Faking it drains our energy and keeps us from facing it. Remember the prodigal son? He ran away before he came to his senses.

The 12-step program is about coming to your senses. Insanity is doing the same thing over and over but expecting different results. If you get on the elevator with someone who works on the twelfth floor and he pushes the tenth floor button every day, gets off and walks up two flights of stairs, you would say, "That's nuts." He needs someone around who is willing to say, "That's nuts." That's like the man who mixes rum with coke and throws it up. Then he says, "There is something wrong with that coke." That's nuts.

Many families would rather look good than tell the truth. They fake it rather than trying to fix it. Most people who have self-destructive, negative behaviors continue these habits because the people around them allow it. They rescue them from the consequences they should suffer from irresponsible behavior. We've found that when people suffer the consequences enough, the pain draws them to the power. They are in so much pain that it drives them to change their lives. Honesty usually doesn't occur unless we experience the pain and hurt from our behavior.

I'll take this a step further. During thousands of hours of counseling with hundreds of people, no one has ever said, "I learned the easy way." They all said, "I learned the hard way." I think most of us learn the hard way. If it isn't hard, we can coast along with what we are doing. Experiencing pain drives us to the power of Christ.

The prodigal son may never have returned to his father if he hadn't experienced the pain of eating with the pigs. During his time of desperation perhaps his father could have rescued his son, using his wealth and connections to get him a decent job. But that would have been unhelpful and even harmful.

When I was in private practice, people called from different parts of the country requesting that I see their child. "If I can just get my son to see you, he will quit drinking." I always told them, "Don't come because he won't be helped." Families think that I can fix the problem. Guess what my success rate is with people like that – zero. People don't change until they are ready to change. The Bible teaches that God can even bring people back from the dead, and some people still won't believe.

You may be thinking, "How can I help someone?" Sometimes the best way to help is to let the person live with the pigs. Breakthrough happens when breakdown occurs. One day he will come to his senses and say, "I'm going home." When he does come home, decide to be the welcoming father and not the elder brother.

Mark or Charles?

Life on the road is interesting. I tell people that I have been in more hotel rooms than Gideon's Bible. Actually, a few weeks ago I was in a Super Motel 4 and they had only half of the Gideon's Bible. One time I was in a hotel that was so bad they stole *my* towels. One of my fears about traveling is arriving at the wrong destination. One time I was scheduled to speak in Odessa, Texas, and thought I was flying into the Midland-Odessa airport. I love to speak in West Texas because the people are lonely. When I arrived at the airport I thought I was in the wrong place. I thought I had messed up big time and flown to the wrong city. After frantically checking with a few people, I learned they had relocated to their new airport since my last visit.

I do worry about flying to the wrong city, but my greatest fear actually happened one time – being the wrong person. As I look back I should have known something was wrong. A few days before I was to speak, the church requested that I sing a few songs at the banquet. The girls in the office thought it was hilarious for anyone to request my singing. They thought someone would one day pay me not to sing but never pay me to sing. They told me about the singing request, and we all laughed and didn't think anything about it. When I arrived, the pastor's first question was "Do you want me to call you Mark or Charles?" I thought that was odd but immediately said, "Charles is fine." I then began to wonder why he asked me that question. I was beginning to get a little nervous but saw my bio on the seat beside him. I glanced at it and it talked about Charles Lowery, Ph.D., Psychologist. I relaxed. Not for long. The pastor told me that we had a mutual friend and, being curious about how he had booked me, I asked him who it was. He told me it was Larnelle Harris, and he knew that we had sung a lot together.

Suddenly, it all comes together – the request to sing, does he call me Mark or Charles, and our mutual friend, Larnelle. I realized that this pastor thinks he has booked Mark Lowry to do his banquet. What do I do? Jump out of the car and run? Pray that he will have a wreck before we get to the church? I know that "the truth will set you free," but I don't work for free. I need this honorarium. As a matter of fact, I need Mark Lowry's honorarium. I figure it's about four times what I get. Finally I say, "You think I'm Mark Lowry, the singer, don't you?" He says "Yes!" I pick up the bio and say, "This is me, Charles the psychologist, not Mark the singer." He says, "I thought you did both." This guy wants Mark the schizophrenic singing psychologist.

We are now sitting at the hotel staring at each other. I asked him if he has advertised that Mark Lowry is coming. He said, "Yes," and I said, "Is there a cliff close for both of us to jump off of?" He isn't laughing. I suggested that I return home and not do the banquet, to which he responds, "You have to do the banquet. What exactly do you do, anyway?" I asked if he remembered Bob Newhart who played the psychologist on TV, and he said he did. "I'm not him either, but I am a shrink and I do make people laugh while teaching them at the same time." He had a glazed look on his face as if he had just eaten ten Krispy Kreme donuts. When I went to my room, I actually read Gideon's Bible. A couple of hours later, a man picked me up for the banquet. He called me Mark. I now had the glazed look on my face and I wished I had ten Krispy Kreme donuts. The pastor's wife greeted me at the door and said how sorry she was about the mix up and assured me that things were going to be okay. The pastor had asked around, and some people had actually heard of me, that I was funny. She said the pastor was pretty relaxed about the whole ordeal. I was thinking that I was glad he was relaxed. I was going to the bathroom every ten minutes.

The banquet went well. After it was over a man came up to me with a tear in his eye and told me that he really needed what I had to say. He had lost his job and was desperately down, but now he was ready to give life another shot. He said, "The pastor thought we needed a singer tonight, but God knew I needed a shrink. I didn't need Mark; I needed you."

As I reflect on that weekend, which I can now do without throwing up, I realize how blessed I am. I tell people how good God is. When I was a young boy I played marbles. I had my roly-polys and black beauties. I really enjoyed the game because I played for keeps. There is always a bully in the neighborhood, though, who will cheat and steal your marbles. One day I realized I had lost my marbles. What do you do when you've lost your marbles? If you have a good father, you go to him and he gets them back. Many people have lost their marbles. I tell them they have a heavenly Father who can get them back. This Father is so good that if there are 100 people and one is lost, he will look for the one that is lost and bring him back.

Many times He sends one of us to bring that one who is lost back home. He may use a banquet or even a book – perhaps this one. He is a good God. His name is Jehovah Jireh. He meets our needs. I also believe he has another name. It is Jehovah Ha Ha, because he must laugh at us in the process.

The Next Level

One key to a great life is to relax in God's goodness.

The other day I flew on American Airlines. On Delta, I'm a Million Miler (I've flown over a million miles with Delta), so at Delta, I'm a hero and they give me special privileges. For instance, I'm usually bumped up to first class, and I love it. I'm a hero with Delta but a zero with American because I don't fly that airline much. So on American I'm back in the coach section – middle seat, 37B. I always seem to get between two nutritionally enhanced people who are running over into my seat. It's amazing. When I sit in first class I think, "I deserve this. I put in the miles, I deserve it." But when I'm in coach class, I walk by first class, look at those people, and think, "Why do they deserve this?" I can get a bad attitude just by walking through first class. Then the flight attendant pulls the curtain, and that ticks me off even more. I smell the food and hear the clanging of dishes and know that the passengers in first class are getting real food.

By the time I arrived at my destination I was tired. It was only an hour and forth-five minute flight and all I did was just sit and drink Diet Coke, but I wore myself out. Why? Because I made myself miserable thinking, "Why am I not up in first class?"

Several years ago Penny and I went to Hawaii. We were having a great time and totally enjoying the trip. A friend had told me that I ought to see a particular hotel on the same island where we were staying, so we went to see the Grand Wailea, and, indeed, it was a spectacular property. After seeing that hotel, I decided that ours was a dump. It almost stole my joy. I had to keep telling myself I was staying at a great place. Don't let the next level destroy your joy.

We had a fund-raising campaign one time, and for the grand prize, I gave away my car. After the campaign I needed a car, so a friend of mine gave me his old Lincoln that was almost as big as a room. I discovered that there are a lot of positive things about driving an old car. For one thing, I don't worry about getting dents and dings. If someone hits my car, it won't hurt. The other day I was at a traffic light, and a guy bumped me from the rear. That would have really upset me in a new car, but being in an old junker, it didn't bother me a bit. He was waving at me. I got out and asked him if he were hurt. He said he was sorry but he didn't have insurance. I looked at his car and realized I was a level up from him. Now don't get me wrong. If God gives me a Jag I'm going to take it and enjoy it and park it way out in the parking lot where you can't put a ding in it. The key is to enjoy your level and to understand what is really important. The stuff is the fluff of life but the basics are the blessings.

Life is like a Hebrew word. It can be understood only by reading it backwards. We go to the end of life and look back. One day you will have a funeral. The family will come and the pastor will say some nice words. After the funeral, your family and friends will all go home and eat potato salad. Life is like Monopoly. You may own property on Boardwalk, or you may be renting on Baltic. It doesn't really matter because in the end it all goes back in the box. The next generation will be getting out all of your stuff and playing with it or fighting over it. To find out what is really important in life, see who shows up at your funeral. The only things that matter are faith, family, and friends.

My wife has heard me tell the potato salad story many times. Not long ago I did the hardest thing I have ever done. I had to tell my five-year-old grandson, Drew, that his two-year-old brother, Jake, was dead. Many people wanted to comfort us. They brought us food and flowers. One day Penny called me to the refrigerator. I noticed she had a tear in her eye. She pointed to the bottom shelf of the refrigerator, and there were two large containers of potato salad. She said, "It happens to everyone. It even happens to us." Then she said, "When you travel around the country and tell the potato salad story, make sure you tell people that if there is someone they should love, they need to love him now. If there is someone they need to forgive, they need to forgive him now."

Many times I've heard the expression "Think outside the box." That may be the most important issue in deciding what is important in life – what lasts outside the box. It is things eternal, not material. Think outside the box, and you will discover the blessings.

When we put little Jake in the box, the world said that it was over. But God says that it was just the beginning. I think of Jake and the box. What keeps me going is that I know that for a while I'm thinking outside the box, and Jake is living outside the box. Thank goodness we serve a God who thinks outside the box, which means there is the next level.

The Prize

An old preacher was on a ship in which the wind was blowing over 100 miles an hour. He started to pray, "God, send us the spirit of the children of Israel, the children of Moses, and the children of the Promised Land." Another brother began to pray, "Lord, don't send nobody. Come yourself, this ain't no time for children." The cross is not really for children. That is why the Mel Gibson movie *The Passion of the Christ* is rated R. The cross is about sin and death and the hurt that it causes.

When our daughter Kasey was about four years old, she fell and hurt her chin on a coffee table. When I arrived, the bleeding had stopped and she was playing with a friend but I knew the cut needed stitches. Our doctor told us to bring her to the emergency room. I told Kasey we needed to go to the hospital to sew up her chin and she told me I didn't understand. Her chin didn't hurt anymore. Have you ever tried reasoning with a four year old? I finally just got on my knees and asked if she knew I loved her. She said yes she did and I told her I would never hurt her but that her chin would never be the same unless it had stitches. Tears came to her eyes and she said "Yes Sir." Being a Psychologist, I promised her that we would go to Kmart for a prize after we went to the hospital. We passed Kmart on the way and she said, "Daddy I have a better idea, why don't we go to Kmart first?" Pretty smart kid. As we walked into the hospital she took my hand and said, "Daddy, hold onto me and don't let me go." The doctor put a papoose on her that looked like a straight jacket to me. She smiled at me and motioned for me to hold her hand. It was a tough situation, and I thought that she wouldn't want anything to do with me for the rest of the day, and she probably wouldn't even go to Kmart with me. But then I felt her hand in mine and she said, "Daddy I love you. Thanks for holding on to me."

My friend, you will go through difficult times and when you do, it's okay to cry. Remember the cross. It means that God is not going to let you go no matter what the circumstances.

When Charleston Heston was filming the movie *Ben Hur*, he was worried about the chariot scene. Finally the director told him to remember that it was a movie and all Heston had to do was just stay on the chariot and keep riding, and the director would make sure he won.

The best I can tell you is that because of the cross, our life is like a movie – God has written the final scene and because of the cross we win the race and He gives us the prize. What a Savior!